The New Deal as a Triumph of Social Work

DOI: 10.1057/9781137527813.0001

Other Palgrave Pivot titles

Nicholas Pamment: Community Reparation for Young Offenders: Perceptions, Policy and Practice

David F. Tennant and Marlon R. Tracey: Sovereign Debt and Credit Rating Bias

Jefferson Walker: King Returns to Washington: Explorations of Memory, Rhetoric, and Politics in the Martin Luther King, Jr. National Memorial

Giovanni Barone Adesi and Nicola Carcano: Modern Multi-Factor Analysis of Bond Portfolios: Critical Implications for Hedging and Investing

Rilka Dragneva and Kataryna Wolczuk: Ukraine between the EU and Russia: The Integration Challenge

Viola Fabbrini, Massimo Guidolin and Manuela Pedio: The Transmission Channels of Financial Shocks to Stock, Bond, and Asset-Backed Markets: An Empirical Analysis

Timothy Wood: Detainee Abuse During Op TELIC: 'A Few Rotten Apples'?

Lars Klüver, Rasmus Øjvind Nielsen and Marie Louise Jørgensen (editors): Policy-Oriented Technology Assessment Across Europe: Expanding Capacities

Rebecca E. Lyons and Samantha J. Rayner (editors): The Academic Book of the Future

Ben Clements: Surveying Christian Beliefs and Religious Debates in Post-War Britain

Robert A. Stebbins: Leisure and the Motive to Volunteer: Theories of Serious, Casual, and Project-Based Leisure

Dietrich Orlow: Socialist Reformers and the Collapse of the German Democratic Republic

Gwendolyn Audrey Foster: Disruptive Feminisms: Raced, Gendered, and Classed Bodies in Film

Catherine A. Lugg: US Public Schools and the Politics of Queer Erasure

Olli Pyyhtinen: More-than-Human Sociology: A New Sociological Imagination

Jane Hemsley-Brown and Izhar Oplatka: Higher Education Consumer Choice

Arthur Asa Berger: Gizmos or: The Electronic Imperative: How Digital Devices have Transformed American Character and Culture

Antoine Vauchez: Democratizing Europe

Cassie Smith-Christmas: Family Language Policy: Maintaining an Endangered Language in the Home

Liam Magee: Interwoven Cities

palgrave▶**pivot**

The New Deal as a Triumph of Social Work: Frances Perkins and the Confluence of Early Twentieth Century Social Work with Mid-Twentieth Century Politics and Government

Stephen Paul Miller
Professor, St. John's University, USA

palgrave
macmillan

DOI: 10.1057/9781137527813.0001

First published in 2016 by
PALGRAVE MACMILLAN®
in the United States—a division of St. Martin's Press LLC,
175 Fifth Avenue, New York, NY 10010.

Where this book is distributed in the UK, Europe and the rest of the world,
this is by Palgrave Macmillan, a division of Macmillan Publishers Limited,
registered in England, company number 785998, of Houndmills,
Basingstoke, Hampshire RG21 6XS.

Palgrave Macmillan is the global academic imprint of the above companies
and has companies and representatives throughout the world.

Palgrave® and Macmillan® are registered trademarks in the United States,
the United Kingdom, Europe and other countries.

ISBN: 978–1–137–52782–0 EPUB
ISBN: 978–1–137–52781–3 PDF
ISBN: 978–1–137–52780–6 Hardback

Library of Congress Cataloging-in-Publication Data is available from
the Library of Congress.

A catalogue record of the book is available from the British Library.

First edition: 2016

www.palgrave.com/pivot

DOI: 10.1057/9781137527813

For my son

DOI: 10.1057/9781137527813.0001

Contents

DOI: 10.1057/9781137527813.0001

Acknowledgments

For her tireless, enthusiastic, and skillful editing and indexing of this book, I thank Jessica A. Wharton. This book was supported by generous grants from St. John's University Summer Support of Research, Recognition, and Research Reduction support; the KlezKanada 2015 Retreat; 2010 New York American Studies Association Summer Institute; and by the New York Public Library for access to the Shoichi Noma Room. I also wish to acknowledge my debt to my son for piquing my interest in Frances Perkins. My thought and research were also significantly aided by Peter Nicholls, Jonathan Alter, Perry Meisel, John Misak, Robert Soto, William Byrne, Arthur L. Miller, Sam Haselby, Marjorie Perloff, Dan Sandford, Matthew Sigelman, Eric Teperman, Susan Reed, Eric Miller, Lehman Weichselbaum, Samuel T. Miller, Moishe Kampin, Thomas Kitts, Ron Kolm, Vidhya Jayaprakash, Maria Duchnowski, Kenneth Deifik, Peter Frank, Jeffrey Kinkley, Joseph Bongiorno, Liz Gross, Mauricio Borrero, Elaine Carey, Timothy A. Milford, Susie J. Pak, Susan Schmidt-Horning, Konrad Tuchscherer, John Lowney, Gabriel E Brownstein, Kathleen Lubey, Raj Chetty, Granville Ganter, Tony Torn, Lee Ann Brown, the New York Public Library Archives and Manuscript Collection, the Columbia University Libraries Archival Collections Frances Perkins Papers 1895–1965, and the Franklin D. Roosevelt Presidential Library in Hyde Park, New York.

palgrave▶**pivot**

www.palgrave.com/pivot

Introduction: The Social Work of Desire

Abstract: *This chapter serves to frame Frances Perkins's social work within the history of economic rights in the United States, highlighting each's considerations of centrifugal and centripetal rights, examining closely the difference between the two. The New Deal's framework coincides with this discussion of personal rights with detailed analysis of the economic mindset of historical figures in shaping FDR's policy and Perkins's social work. By providing background to the New Deal, particularly in its social work underpinnings, the chapter puts it in the context of the history of personal rights in America and in Perkins's perspective.*

Keywords: bread and roses; Civilian Conservation Corps; economic rights; Frankin Roosevelt; Government Work Program; New Deal; Otis L. Graham Jr; progressive; Rose Schneiderman; Triangle Fire Commission; United States Employment Service; Works Project Administration

Miller, Stephen Paul. *The New Deal as a Triumph of Social Work: Frances Perkins and the Confluence of Early Twentieth Century Social Work with Mid-Twentieth Century Politics and Government.* New York: Palgrave Macmillan, 2016. DOI: 10.1057/9781137527813.0003.

Early twentieth century social workers, says New Deal historian Otis Graham, are not only the most enthusiastic New Deal supporters remaining from the Progressive Era. They are, surprisingly, the only Progressive Era survivors who are uniformly enthusiastic about the New Deal. The New Deal, says Graham, "satisf[ies] the most deeply rooted *desire*" of the early social workers (italics added).[1] And yet for Frances Perkins all social work is of desire since for her no change occurs unless "desire[d] deeply in an emotional way."[2]

Secretary of Labor Perkins and President Franklin Roosevelt see economic rights as a social work of desire in two ways. First, a desire to eradicate debilitating poverty shields Perkins from the ideological blinders obstructing most American progressives and conservatives from seeing startlingly practical solutions close at hand which would be obvious if it were not for a widespread insistence that such solutions are impossible. The Depression's demands aside, Perkins wishes to institute something like an ongoing Works Project Administration (WPA), in effect educating workers in basic skills, guaranteeing workplace opportunities, and obliterating so-called cultures and mindsets of poverty.[3] And yet this first sense of the "social work of desire" is more conventional than the second sense of the term, since the second sense does not apply to what we normally think of as an economic right—a right that is usually thought of as one's right to a minimal subsistence.

The second sense of "a social work of desire" reflects how FDR's articulations of economic rights guarantee not only the right to survive but also the right to flourish by contributing to the economic life of the nation. Rose Schneiderman, the labor secretary whose oratory Perkins says inspires her to address the social inequities underlying the Triangle Shirtwaist Factory fire, similarly speaks of the rights of workers, particularly the rights of women workers, to live with both "bread and roses," that is, the right not only to survive but also to live a decent and an enriching civic and domestic life.[4] This is impossible, says Schneiderman, when work leaves one "too weary for anything but supper and bed." "Romance needs time," Schneiderman wryly adds. "What the woman who labors wants is the right to live, not simply exist—the right to life as the rich woman has it, the right to life, and the sun, and music, and art," asserts Schneiderman in 1912. She says to the wealthy, "You have nothing that the humblest worker has not a right to have also. The worker must have

DOI: 10.1057/9781137527813.0003

bread, but she must have roses, too."[5] Interestingly, James Oppenheim writes a poem based on Schneiderman's phrase describing a worker's right to "Bread and Roses" and several musicians have since put the poem to music in a number of songs, performed by Joan Baez, Ani DiFranco, John Denver, Judy Collins, John Lucker, Renate Fresow, Utah Phillips, and many others. This reemergence of Schneiderman's sentiment of the 1910s in the 1960s reflects how the "roses" aspect of economic rights becomes a subject of 1960s aspiration that though unfulfilled is not set aside.

In 1930 Governor Franklin Roosevelt tells Perkins that to do "the best politics" she should not "say anything about politics. Just be an outraged social worker and scientist."[6] Perkins brings to politics an alternative and apolitical social worker's perspective in this regard.

Perkins never expects to serve in government. She is stunned to find herself steering the Triangle Fire commission: "I was a young person then and certainly not fit for service on any super commission but I was the chief."[7] Nonetheless, Perkins's deft use of social work skills alters American government through several innovative methods, morphing early twentieth century social work into arguably the first truly modern government.

As U.S. Labor Secretary, Perkins stresses the Labor Department's role as an "employment service" for hiring within the Civilian Conservation Corps (CCC), Federal Emergency Relief Administration (FERA), and WPA: "Somebody had to certify these people," says Perkins. "When they lined up wanting a job, we had to put them through the employment service.... Most of the employees in the National Re-Employment did heroic work.... Out of the National Re-Employment Service were themselves men out of work—men and women.... They developed people whom we later...found suitable for employment in the USES [United States Employment Service]. They worked in and have been there ever since.... That's how I kept so close to the details of the relief program. Through the employment service, the people going on the relief works were passing through our hands."[8]

Perkins considers her role in organizing New Deal emergency relief government work programs a typical social work task. "I continued my interest in [the WPA], first, because I was a professional social worker." The WPA, notes Perkins, is "magnificent" social work.[9]

DOI: 10.1057/9781137527813.0003

Notes

1　Otis L. Graham, Jr., *Encore for Reform?: The Old Progressives and the New Deal* (New York: Oxford University Press, 1967), p. 103.
2　Columbia University Libraries Oral History Research Office, "Frances Perkins," Part 2, p. 49, available at http://www.columbia.edu/cu/lweb/digital/collections/nny/perkinsf/toc.html
3　Frances Perkins, *The Roosevelt I Knew* (New York: The Viking Press, 1946), pp. 189–190.
4　Eisenstein, *Give Us Bread but Give Us Roses: Working Women's Consciousness in the United States, 1890 to the First World War* (London: Routledge, 1983), p. 32.
5　Ibid.
6　George Martin, *Madam Secretary: Frances Perkins* (Boston: Houghton Mifflin, 1976), p. 218.
7　Frances Perkins, Lecture on September 30, 1964 at Cornell University, School of Industrial and Labor Relations. Lectures of Frances Perkins, Collection /3047, 30 September 1964, Cornell University, Kheel Center for Labor-Management Documentation and Archives, Ithaca, NY, http://trianglefire.ilr.cornell.edu/primary/lectures/FrancesPerkinsLecture.html?CFID=539880&CFTOKEN=77298054
8　Columbia University Libraries, Part 4, pp. 532–534.
9　Columbia University Libraries, Part 4, p. 532.

1
Bold, Persistent Social Work

Abstract: *The pathway to Frances Perkins's career in social work and government combines empirical observation and scientific method with quirky pragmatism and personal commitment. The era before social work practice is codified stamps both Perkins's mode of work and the New Deal's "temper [of] bold, persistent experimentation" [Franklin D. Roosevelt, "Address at Oglethorpe University in Atlanta, Georgia, May 22, 1932]. This chapter outlines Perkins' personal history, ranging from her initial encounters with poverty to her reading of Riis's* How the Other Half Lives, *which inspires her to do something about the poor. Perkins's experiences in Chicago's Hull House, Philadelphia Research and Protective Association, and National Consumers League, in addition to her investigation of the Triangle Fire, prepare her to help shape New York State and national government and the New Deal.*

Keywords: Abraham Flexner; Annah May Soule; Charity Organization Society; Chicago Commons; Edward T. Devine; Florence Kelley; Hull House; Jacob Riis; Jane Addams; John Dewey; National Consumers League; Philadelphia Research and Protective Association; Settlement houses; Triangle Fire

Miller, Stephen Paul. *The New Deal as a Triumph of Social Work: Frances Perkins and the Confluence of Early Twentieth Century Social Work with Mid-Twentieth Century Politics and Government.* New York: Palgrave Macmillan, 2016.
DOI: 10.1057/9781137527813.0004.

Frances Perkins might not have become a social worker had she not observed factory workers while doing fieldwork for her Mount Holyoke College sociology course. Perkins becomes aware of the plights of working, disabled, and unemployed Americans. Although she majors in chemistry and physics at Mount Holyoke from 1898 to 1902, she intermingles her interest in scientific investigation with a budding personal commitment to social reform informed by empirical observation and the social sciences.

Perkins's studies challenge her social preconceptions. She learns new approaches to social reform utilizing fledgling social sciences. At a time when the study of history emphasizes "great men," Perkins's American history professor, Annah May Soule, takes her classes to nearby factories to collect data about working conditions. Soule acquaints Perkins with a scientifically rigorous and experiential approach to "social studies."

This method familiarizes Perkins with poor industrial workers. Perkins's parents, though "charitable," do not consider the possibility of larger social conditions relating to poverty.[1] The young Perkins also assumes that poverty is merely a symptom of alcoholism, laziness, or overspending.[2] However, in Soule's class Perkins sees how the absence of workers' compensation can turn one person's accident into an entire family's poverty. At textile and paper mills, Perkins witnesses factory work's hazards, child labor, long hours, low pay, and unjust wage disparity for women and children.[3] Perkins concludes that poverty *does* have social causes, and when Jacob Riis's *How the Other Half Lives* publicizes abject big city poverty, Perkins feels personally challenged by Riis's question to his readers: "What are you going to do about it?"[4]

Perkins finds answers to Riis's query when Florence Kelley visits Mount Holyoke in February 1902. Kelley shows how Soule's social science methodology can be applied to social work.[5] Like many educated women of Perkins's generation with limited career choices, Perkins feels "formless" in her professional "aspirations"[6] before discovering Kelley's "program...for industrial and human and social justice" which molds her "aspirations for social justice into some definite purpose."[7] In several years, Kelley's program leads to Perkins working for Kelley's National Consumers League in New York.

Perkins credits Kelley with showing her "the work which became my vocation."[8] Kelley makes becoming a social worker seem possible.[9] After graduating Perkins seeks employment at the Charity Organization Society of New York, but the organization's head, Edward T. Devine,

DOI: 10.1057/9781137527813.0004

suggests she first "gain some life experience," and Perkins teaches in several Connecticut and Massachusetts schools, eventually teaching physics and biology at a wealthy boarding school near Chicago in Lake Forest, Illinois.[10]

Perkins's proximity to Chicago allows her to work at Chicago Commons and live at Jane Addams's Hull House, two early settlement houses. Addams's establishment of the first American settlement house makes Addams, in the words of Arthur M. Schlesinger, Jr., "the first heroine of social work".[11] Hull House, and the settlement houses following it, says Schlesinger, "gave the middle class its first extended contact with the life of the working class."[12] Social workers live with the poor at settlement houses in immigrant neighborhoods. Comfortable middle class Americans, such as Perkins, personally experience the degradation and drudgery of sweatshops, unregulated child labor, unsafe and unclean work environments, and suppression of unions and collective bargaining.

Hull House distributes vital goods and services no government agency offers, such as food, medical care, health services, educational classes, childcare and kindergarten, job training, library services, banking, employment, shelter for the homeless and abused,[13] and instruction in the English language and becoming an American citizen.[14] Also significantly, Hull House provides homes and meeting places for those researching poverty and its causes, thus triggering creative synergy amongst reformers seeking solutions.[15] This feature of Hull House and other settlement houses influences Perkins throughout her career in social work and government, and helps her develop the "conference method" as a tool for investigating the Triangle Fire. Her first prolonged social work experience emphasizes "the intense vitality," "intrinsic optimism," and "self-confidence bolstered by optimism" that Kirsten Downey recognizes in both Frances Perkins and Franklin Roosevelt.[16] This persistent vitality and optimism is a hallmark of Perkins's social work that later reverberates within Roosevelt's presidency.

Perkins quits teaching to become a fulltime volunteer at Hull House in 1906. In 1907, she begins working for a small nonprofit organization, the Philadelphia Research and Protective Association. In her first social work job, she demonstrates a bold persistence that twenty-five years later she brings to Washington.

In Perkins's first paid social work job, she helps dismantle sexual slavery operations. One might expect government to be in the forefront

DOI: 10.1057/9781137527813.0004

of remedying such a serious social problem, and Perkins does in fact need to appeal to the Philadelphia municipal government for help. Nonetheless, the need for Perkins, as a social worker, to take the lead in these investigations indicates how government has changed since then.

For this job, Perkins jokes that she has no formal social work "training" and yet "began at the top."[17] Indeed, she is the Association's only paid employee. In a sense she has no superiors although she earns so little she needs to ask advice about how to eat on a meager budget from the poor women whom she helps. With little supervision, Perkins does every significant part of the Philadelphia Research and Protective Association's work from managing the office and fundraising to social research and investigation to writing up reports and taking actions based upon them.[18]

There is then little agreement about how to train a social worker, and it is difficult to train or supervise Perkins in a professional manner. However, Perkins's strengths as a government administrator are fashioned by her background as a social worker at a time before social work is professionalized.

In the early twentieth century, social work's status as a valid profession is suspect. The social work of objective and impartial study seems at loggerheads with social work that functions through personal contact with individuals and advocacy of causes. Social workers are then often viewed more as volunteer charity workers than professionals.

In 1915, Abraham Flexner concludes that social work is not a profession since it lacks a teachable skill-set.[19] Social workers are conflicted. Steven J. Diner notes that "tensions between" "the desire for advocacy" and "scholarly objectivity" play out among turn of the twentieth century social workers, between those believing their primary task to be the "alleviation" of "the causes of social problems" and "the treatment of victims of social ills" and those more concerned with studying "social welfare" and "social work practice."[20]

Perkins admits that she and other early social workers are working largely in the dark. However, she feels that social work can be both a social mindset and a practical science. Perkins develops "a conviction, a 'concern,' as the Quakers say, about social justice; and it was clear in [her] own mind that the promotion of social justice could be made practical."[21] Perkins does not define social work, but she characterizes it as an activity in keeping with the Progressive Era's spirit of social reform before social work "had become so professionalized. We were all amateurs. We

DOI: 10.1057/9781137527813.0004

were doing professional jobs, but we hadn't had any special training," recalls Perkins about early social workers. "We saw poverty and went in to relieve it in all kinds of *odd ways*" (italics added).[22]

For Perkins, social reform suggests a "conviction that something ought to be done."[23] This conviction comes from an awareness of social problems, and it vigorously interacts with "all kinds of odd ways" to solve them. Because Perkins thinks mentors such as Addams and Kelley have an "enormous influence" on society, Perkins "never believe[s] in" destructive "social 'forces'—economic, political or anything else" as givens. She is not a fatalist. To the contrary, her observations confirm her radical optimism. "I think that fifty people," Perkins says, "with a determination to do something right can start forces that have their strength largely because of the moral appeal of what it is that they're recommending," and if fifty people who can see the world as it is can change it, all social problems can be solved.[24]

Perkins views social work as a dynamic activity. Rigidly formulaic social work training misses the point of social work because for Perkins social work has such a wide range of possible activity and concerns everyone. To some extent everyone is a social worker. Given her tendency to learn by doing, in keeping with educational models that John Dewey popularizes in the early twentieth century, it is not surprising that before Perkins studies social work at a university or college, she experiences great success *doing* social work.

Working as the only Philadelphia Research and Protective Association employee, Perkins almost single-handedly battles the kidnapping and forced prostitution of immigrant and newly arriving African American women. She diagnoses the problem by researching "lodging houses, transportation facilities, wages, employment offices, types of jobs, social connections, and the legal system." Better zoning and withholding of licenses to the illegitimate housing provided for the women are critical in eradicating the problem. More Philadelphia police at the docks when the young women arrive in the city is also crucial. Perkins also knows it is vital that she make contacts within the corrupt Republican Philadelphia government to implement these solutions.[25]

Perkins befriends the victimized women. In so doing, she endangers herself. "I look at it now and realize that it was a very risky and a bold thing for me to be in—a young girl who knew nothing," recalls Perkins.[26] At one point she is followed by two men whom she "had tried to put out of the employment" and is investigating. Perkins protects herself by

DOI: 10.1057/9781137527813.0004

screaming the name of one of the men following her. She also uses an umbrella. "They increased their pace to catch up with me and I turned suddenly and they ran right into my umbrella," Perkins recalls. "It was a sudden turn and I then screamed. I called the man's name—his name was Sam Smith. I remember it to this day. He kept the most terrible, cheating employment office... They turned and ran. It gave me the feeling that if you put up a bold front people will turn and run... You can't run and let them stab you."[27] Such quick thinking expresses the adventure implicit in early social work. Perkins draws upon the courage, resourcefulness, and guile she learns as a young social worker in her subsequent career in government.

In 1932, Franklin Roosevelt promises government that is "bold, persistent," and "brave."[28] What is bold about the New Deal often corresponds on a larger scale with the daring of early social workers. In Perkins's first social work job, she accordingly shows boldness, persistence, and bravery as integral to social work in the first decade of the twentieth century. She also learns investigative skills to gather sufficient information to persuade the government to help cure a serious social problem. Her second social work job hones these skills into a discernible "method of moral progress."[29] In this method, investigative and persuasive social work skills are harnessed to move government to enact laws.

Notes

1   Naomi Pasachoff, *Frances Perkins: The Coming of the New Deal* (New York: Oxford University Press, 1999), p. 14.
2   Martin, pp. 50–51.
3   Penny Coleman, *A Woman Unafraid: The Achievements of Frances Perkins* (New York: Asja Press, 2010), p. 11.
4   Pasachoff, p. 16.
5   Martin, p. 53.
6   Pasachoff, p. 15.
7   Martin, p. 230.
8   Ibid., p. 52.
9   Adam Cohen, *Nothing To Fear* (New York: Penguin Press, 2009), p. 163.
10   Pasachoff, pp. 15–17.
11   Arthur M. Schlesinger, Jr., *The Age Of Roosevelt, Volume I, 1919–1933: The Crisis of the Old Order* (Boston: Houghton Mifflin Company, 1957), p. 22.
12   Ibid., pp. 22–23.

DOI: 10.1057/9781137527813.0004

13 Cohen, pp. 164–165.

14 Kirstin Downey, *The Woman Behind the New Deal: The Life and Legacy of Frances Perkins, Social Security, Unemployment Insurance, and the Minimum Wage* (New York, Random House, 2009), p. 19.

15 Steven Diner, "Scholarship in the Quest for Social Welfare: A Fifty-Year History of the Social Service Review," *Social Service Review*, 51:1 (March, 1977): 2–3.

16 Downey, p. 49.

17 Ibid., pp. 19–22.

18 Coleman, p. 18.

19 Dan Hoff, "Social Casework," in *Progress and Reform: A Cyberhistory* http://www.socialworkhistorystation.org/history/chapts/4-2b.htm.

20 Diner, p. 66.

21 Perkins, *Roosevelt*, p. 10.

22 Columbia University Libraries, ch. 1, pp. 168–169.

23 Ibid., p. 168.

24 Ibid.

25 Coleman, p. 17.

26 Columbia University Libraries, ch. 1, p. 31.

27 Ibid., pp. 31–32.

28 University of California at Santa Barbara, The American Presidency Project, Franklin D. Roosevelt, Address at Ogelthorpe University in Atlanta, GA, May 22, 1932. http://www.presidency.ucsb.edu/ws/?pid=88410 (accessed May 6, 2013).

29 Frances Perkins, "A Method of Moral Progress," *New Republic*, 129:8 (June 8, 1953): 18–19.

DOI: 10.1057/9781137527813.0004

2
A Method of Moral Progress

Abstract: *After a discussion about Perkins's social work in Philadelphia, this chapter focuses on Simon Patten's influence on Perkins. Like Patten, Perkins does not view labor as a mere commodity or expense; she believes all work can promote dignity. This chapter discusses Perkins's experience with the Consumers League in addition to the League's history of influencing policy by working within government itself.*

Keywords: Brandeis Brief; Consumer's League; Simon Patten; Volstead Act

Miller, Stephen Paul. *The New Deal as a Triumph of Social Work: Frances Perkins and the Confluence of Early Twentieth Century Social Work with Mid-Twentieth Century Politics and Government*. New York: Palgrave Macmillan, 2016. DOI: 10.1057/9781137527813.0005.

DOI: 10.1057/9781137527813.0005

As a Philadelphia social worker, Perkins wishes to learn "the whole field of social work."[1] Perkins respects social work as a new way of organizing academic knowledge to assist social reform. However, her love of the social sciences is not confined to a strict definition of social work. Perkins is beginning to associate social work with Florence Kelley's "method of moral progress," a method applicable to all manner of social situations.

Upon the advice of her friend and colleague, Mary Ellen Richmond, Perkins attends the Wharton School of Economics at the University of Pennsylvania in 1908 and 1909.[2] Perkins says she "lapped" up courses in economics and sociology.[3] If Annah May Soule is Perkins's most influential Mount Holyoke professor, Perkins's thinking as a graduate student is most informed by University of Pennsylvania economy professor Simon Patten.

Perkins considers Patten "one of the greatest men America has yet produced."[4] Whereas Soule teaches Perkins social science research procedures, Patten contextualizes how social work can develop within industrial society. He introduces Perkins to ideas about industry's ever-growing capacity for production, later helping Perkins counteract those in the Roosevelt administration arguing for strictly balanced budgets.[5] Patten precedes John Maynard Keynes in outlining an economic theory in which the stimulation of consumption spurs production while reducing production costs.[6]

Patten theorizes that modern industrialization's increased per capita production is creating a "surplus civilization," in which poverty can be eliminated and class strife significantly reduced.[7] Patten's notion of surplus civilization makes social justice seem attainable. According to Patten, the very industrialization that has caused poverty and degradation can cure those problems and foster a more humane society. He believes charities and social workers can be replaced with government workers paid by tax revenues stemming from an ever-increasing tax-base provided by industrial wealth.[8] Interestingly, Perkins will become a social worker employed by the government. Patten forecasts "a new kind of charity" that will not subtract from a society's energies or resources nor "create a parasitic class" but rather "distribute the surplus in ways that will promote welfare and secure better preparation for the future."[9]

Patten teaches that labor itself should be of value to the laborer, increasing a worker's value to him or herself so as to develop that worker's potential and humanity.[10] In 1930, Perkins is still developing Patten's ideas when she identifies "government's final job in relation to industry" as making "human welfare" a requisite "manufactured good"

DOI: 10.1057/9781137527813.0005

of "civilized industrial society." In other words, a central "product" of work would one day be the workers' human development and welfare.[11] "Industry and government must turn to the psychologist and the educator to work out certain definite but very simple principles," says Patten, "mak[ing] industrial life educative as well as productive.... Through making something with your hands, 'creative expression' so to speak, real educational experience comes.... Industry is, therefore, the best of all fields of education, because industry is fundamentally a creative process.... The educational aspects of industrial life to-day have not been considered or developed. But if so many of us are going to spend the greater part of our lives in industry, our working time should be a good time, not just an arid waste between brief periods of leisure activity."[12]

Like Patten, Perkins does not view labor as a mere commodity or expense but as an end in itself. She believes all work can promote dignity, a connection to community, and learning. "We talk about labor costs and the fact that we must reduce labor costs. That means that you must treat the man as though he were the iron or the wood that went into the article," says Perkins. "This treating the man and his work as though it were a part of the cost of making the article puts a man on a less than human plane."[13] Perkins's thinking about labor is thereafter rooted in what Meredith A. Newman calls Perkins's "singular focus on the *human* nature of work."[14] Industrialization, after all, can enrich everyone and make labor an avenue toward individual growth, learning, and enjoyment.[15]

Patten encourages Perkins to apply for a Russell Sage Foundation fellowship that he helps her to attain. The fellowship makes it possible for her to move to New York in the summer of 1909 and earn an MA in political science from Columbia University. She graduates in June 1910 upon completing her master's thesis, "A Study of Malnutrition in 107 Children from Public School 51," which concerned malnutrition and other aspects of the poor working and living conditions of immigrants in New York's Hell's Kitchen.[16]

Perkins's reputation is enhanced when she publishes her thesis in the journal *Survey*, and in 1910 the New York chapter of the National Consumers' League hires Perkins. Florence Kelley had founded the National Consumers' League in 1899. Unlike most social work organizations, the League does not directly aid individuals. In this way it resembles the small organization that Perkins works for in Philadelphia. The Consumers League drafts and advocates legislation to achieve social reform.

DOI: 10.1057/9781137527813.0005

The League's activities exemplify one way of professionalizing social work. As its name suggests, the National Consumers League organizes consumers. Kelley wishes to change customary ways of thinking about relations amongest consumers, workers, and employers. Recalling "an old aunt who ate no sugar and wore no cotton because they were slave produced," Kelley asserts reasons that consumers of goods made in sweatshops under abusive work conditions can be said to "employ" poor workers.[17] Kelley reasons that by organizing consumers, particularly wealthy ones with purchasing power, citizens can in effect act as government regulators. The League attempts to make businesses that provide their employees with humane working conditions a workplace standard by granting them a "passing" Consumers League Code and issuing labels for garments affirming that those businesses did not abuse their employees. Consumers are encouraged to boycott businesses without an acceptable League Code.[18]

However, the National Consumers League's focus on enacting legislation has the greatest effect. The League investigates production conditions such as child labor and "homework," which forces workers to take work home and thus extend their work hours and render their homes unsafe workplaces. After a thorough investigation, the League sends out speakers to publicize its research and, in Schlesinger's words, "Stir the public conscience."[19] The League then enlists lawyers to write legislation addressing the social problems it encounters and lobbyists to advocate for that legislation's enactment.

The Consumers League lets Perkins develop the investigatory skills she acquired during her first social work experiences in Philadelphia and Chicago. She begins her work for the Consumers League by investigating unsafe and unsanitary working conditions that include fire hazards in New York's many neighborhood bakeries. Perkins becomes a workplace safety and fire prevention expert. The Consumers League places Perkins in a position in which she is perfectly suited to investigate the Triangle Shirtwaist Factory fire when it occurs. At the time of the Triangle Fire, Perkins is already writing reports about fire safety, especially after twenty-six people die in a Newark workplace fire a year before the Triangle Fire.

Perkins calls Kelley's devotion to social reform through investigation, research, and legislation a "method of moral progress." "Florence Kelley," says Perkins, "was the inventor of a method of moral progress and the catalytic agent of the series of actions which has accomplished so much for the welfare of the nation.... It was her basic principle, which has been

DOI: 10.1057/9781137527813.0005

followed ever since by the most successful social work organizations that investigations and a marshalling of the facts bearing upon the problems must precede any recommendation for legislation or for action."[20]

Two years before Perkins begins working for the Consumers League this method is reinforced by one of the League's most celebrated victories. In 1908, the League persuades future Supreme Court justice Louis Brandeis to write a legal brief relying more on scientific and objective truth than legal precedent. Most of the "Brandeis Brief" consists of testimony by social scientists and health experts supporting an Oregon law limiting the number of hours a week that a woman can work. *Muller v. Oregon* challenges the state law in the Supreme Court. A scientific brief is thought necessary because in 1905 the Supreme Court strikes down a similar New York State law, ruling that it violates the constitutional freedom of contract. The Brandeis Brief's Brief's seemingly scientific (if not by current standards) demonstration of the gender specific harm done to women through overwork sways the court. The Brandeis Brief begins a trend culminating a half-century later in *Brown v. Board of Education*, overturning the legality of public school segregation due to social scientists' testimony about the psychological harm racial segregation inflicts.

At the beginning of the twentieth century, it is not assumed that research and fact can aid in solving social problems. "A century ago," says David Von Drehle, "the idea of tackling social problems by collecting facts—as opposed to scriptural passages or philosophical tenets—was groundbreaking."[21] Social reform does not always appeal to science. For instance, the Volstead Act outlawing the sale of alcohol is also argued to be a vehicle of social reform, but it is not scientifically researched. Such legislation's conclusions tend to be predetermined. Advocates of the Volstead Act, such as the Women's Christian Temperance Union, never cast themselves as disinterested investigators and are more likely to base rationales for their legislation in Scripture than science.[22]

The Brandeis Brief helps ensconce the National Consumers League's method of social reform within the workings of the government itself. The League's mode of producing legislation by identifying social problems, spurring the public's demand to fix them, and drafting and advocating legislation to solve these problems creates a context for Perkins to influence government and eventually join it. It is also a haven for Perkins to continue to do social work that applies science. The Consumers League helps to professionalize social work in a manner that suits Perkins.

DOI: 10.1057/9781137527813.0005

Notes

1   Martin, pp. 493–494.
2   Columbia University Libraries, Part 1, p. 36.
3   Ibid.
4   Arthur M. Schlesinger, Jr., *The Age Of Roosevelt, Volume II, 1933–1935: The Coming of the New Deal* (Boston: Houghton Mifflin Company, 1958), p. 299.
5   Martin, pp. 493–494.
6   Lillian Holman Mohr, *Frances Perkins: "That Woman in FDR's Cabinet!"* (Barrington, MA: North River Press, 1979), p. 30.
7   Martin, p. 72.
8   Ibid., p. 494.
9   Mohr, p. 31.
10 Coleman, p. 18.
11 Frances Perkins, "Helping Industry to Help Itself." *Harper's*, 161 (October 1930): 630.
12 Ibid., p. 629.
13 University Libraries, Part 1, p. 74.
14 Meredith A. Newman, "Madame Secretary Frances Perkins," in Claire Felbinger and Wendy Haynes (eds), *Outstanding Women in Public Administration: Leaders, Mentors, and Pioneers*, pp. 83–102 (New York: M.E. Sharpe Inc., 2004), p. 84.
15 Coleman, p. 18.
16 Martin, pp. 72–74.
17 Perkins, "Method," p. 18.
18 Mohr, p. 38.
19 Schlesinger, vol. I, p. 23.
20 Ibid, p. 19.
21 David Von Drehle, *Triangle: The Fire That Changed America* (New York: Grove Press, 2003), p. 197.
22 Cohen, p. 165.

DOI: 10.1057/9781137527813.0005

3

The Fifty-Four-Hour Bill and Social Work's Alternative Professionalization

Abstract: *This chapter focuses on Perkins's central role in passing the Fifty-Four Hour Bill while working for the Consumers League and her two notable achievements while there. Her influence is shown through her work with Senator McManus on the bill, and the chapter outlines her determination to help the needy through such work. Her alliance with Tammany Hall illustrates her pragmatism and ability to achieve the ends of social work while also aiding Tammany. Through working with government, Perkins resists a growing conservative trend within the social work profession.*

Keywords: Abraham Epstein; Abraham Flexner; Al Smith; Charles Murphy; Consumers League; Fifty-Four-Hour Bill; Florence Kelley; Hartley House; Hell's Kitchen Charity Organization Service; Mary Ellen Richmond; Robert F. Wagner; Stephen Wise; Tammany Hall; Thomas J. McManus; Tim Sullivan

Miller, Stephen Paul. *The New Deal as a Triumph of Social Work: Frances Perkins and the Confluence of Early Twentieth Century Social Work with Mid-Twentieth Century Politics and Government.* New York: Palgrave Macmillan, 2016.
DOI: 10.1057/9781137527813.0006.

 DOI: 10.1057/9781137527813.0006

Perkins plays a central role in two major social reforms while she works for the National Consumers League: her investigation of the Triangle Fire and her lobbying for the Fifty-Four-Hour Bill. Her role in both events demonstrates the ingenuity and determination that she displays during her first job in Philadelphia yet also shows the skills of an innovative new brand of social work influencing government.

While working for the League from 1910 to 1912, she is celebrated for her investigation of the Triangle Shirtwaist Factory fire. However, her success in lobbying for the passage of a New York State maximum-hour workweek law for women and children, the Fifty-Four-Hour Bill, or the Jackson-McManus Bill, also advances social reform and earns headlines and other notoriety for Perkins such as the article "Behind the Rail: Being the Story of a Woman Lobbyist," published in *Metropolitan Magazine.*[1]

Perkins's work for the Fifty-Four-Hour Bill brings her desire to achieve the ends of social work into direct conflict with prevailing social work ideology and practice. The way that Perkins meets the chief sponsor of the Fifty-Four-Hour Bill in the New York State Senate, State Senator Thomas J. McManus, illustrates how Perkins's drive to help the needy leads her away from social work's customary avenues of reform. Social work had after all then become closely associated with Progressive Era efforts to establish more democratic and less corrupt government. Although there is no indication that Perkins is corrupt in any manner she sees the importance of working with "undoubtedly corrupt politicians."[2]

Perkins's introduction to McManus in 1909 is a career-altering experience leading to the realization that solutions to social work problems are found less in ideology than in concrete results. While living at Hartley House, a settlement house in New York's Hell's Kitchen, when she meets a poor family of "Hartley House people" in "awful distress." The family's teenage son has been arrested, and he is, "the sole support of his mother and two little sisters, who," says Perkins, "were obviously nice children.[3]

Before they lose their home, fellow social workers at Hartley House tell Perkins to go to the Hell's Kitchen Charity Organization Service office to secure monetary assistance for the family. Although settlement house workers vouch for the family, "it took them a long time to make the investigation," while Perkins and a few of her friends give the family money. In the meantime, she finds the social work agency's behavior unsettling. "I thought they ought to believe me when I told them about this case," she says.[4]

DOI: 10.1057/9781137527813.0006

When the report finally arrives, it infuriates Perkins. The social work agency's investigation determines that "the mother was somewhat less than worthy—she drank a good deal, had had some very bad lapses in her life, and it was just possible that one of the children was not legitimate." The charity organization refuses the case. It would not help the family because "they just didn't see how they could handle that as one of their cases at all. They couldn't reconstruct that kind of a family."[5] Perkins does not expect the agency's moral judgment to curtail its professed "purpose"—"to give out handouts to the needy."[6]

Perkins knows the family will become destitute without its only wage earner. As a last resort she goes to see State Senator Thomas McManus, the neighborhood's Tammany leader. In the smoky Hell's Kitchen Democratic Tammany clubhouse, Perkins finds an unlikely alternative to the social work agency. At the Ninth Avenue headquarters of Thomas McManus, nicknamed "The McManus" or "The" for short, the senator is cordial to Perkins, agrees with her point of view, and, in a way that she cannot understand, has the boy released from jail the next day.[7] Although McManus is said to be corrupt, as is generally the case with Philadelphia's corrupt Republican political establishment, he is adept at delivering constituate services that Perkins equates with exemplary social work.

Perkins's recruitment of Tammany Hall into her social work causes is an extension of the "odd ways" Perkins says early social workers combat injustice. Such creative advocacy also occurs in her use of social and professional contacts she makes through the Consumers League and elsewhere. For instance, when the Bloomingdale family department store proprietors oppose the Fifty-Four-Hour Bill, Perkins tells the Bloomingdale's rabbi, Stephen Wise, a prominent progressive voice who later supports Franklin Roosevelt. The rabbi reprimands the Bloomingdale brothers and helps convert them into Perkins's allies.[8]

Perkins's alliance with Tammany Hall demonstrates a creative pragmatism. "The distinction of the New Deal lay precisely in its refusal to approach social problems in terms of ideology.... For Roosevelt, the technique of liberal government was pragmatism," says Arthur M. Schlesinger, Jr.[9] Perkins's flexibility and pragmatism contribute to another key tool that she uses repeatedly throughout her career: her unusual ability to unwittingly cause politicians to let her into their confidences and unexpectedly provide her with critical information about important political matters. This might seem like a quality that

DOI: 10.1057/9781137527813.0006

is difficult to place within a historical context. However, instances of it figure so prominently for Perkins that it is reasonable to postulate it as a consequence of Perkins exercising her skill-set as a social worker within a political environment. For instance, in the below discussion of Perkins's lobbying for the Fifty-Four-Hour Bill, both Assemblyman Alfred Smith and State Senator Tim Sullivan surprise Perkins with vital information. The bill certainly would not pass without Sullivan's disclosure. Perkins's ability to get others to confide in her in crucial ways later figures in the unprecedented and secret advice that two Supreme Court Justices give her while crafting the 1935 Social Security Act.

What Perkins learns from her first encounter with The McManus is reinforced three years later in 1912 with the passage of the Fifty-Four-Hour Bill, establishing a workweek hours ceiling for New York's women and children. As in Perkins's first meeting with McManus, passing the Fifty-Four-Hour Bill requires Perkins to again choose pragmatic political wisdom outside social work's customary moral scope. Her choice forces her to play high stakes political poker to beat back overt political opposition, covert parliamentary schemes, and internal division within the Consumers League. The passing of the bill hinges on Perkins's Tammany allies volunteering confidential information to Perkins and offering their expert parliamentary assistance, and her decision to accept their help instead of abiding by the rigid ideals of her social work superiors.

The New York Consumers League lobbies for the Fifty-Four-Hour Bill for three years, during which time the bill is stalled in a New York Assembly committee. Perkins works steadily for the bill's passage for about a year and half. She spends several consecutive months living and lobbying fulltime in Albany on two occasions. State legislators such as Smith, Sullivan, McManus, and State Senator Robert F. Wagner, according to Smith, take her increasingly more seriously as they witness the long hours she dedicates to her cause, the strength of her arguments against the overworking of women and children, and the League's success in popularizing the bill through lead speakers and the press.[10]

Perkins lobbies for the goals of social work to the legislature, but she also provides a way for government and politics to make use of social work. Tammany's leaders see political opportunity in working with Perkins.

In 1910 John Alden Dix is elected as the first Democratic governor since 1891. Dix's victory results from a bitter internal dispute among Republicans followed by a Republican State Senate scandal involving kickbacks and, more seriously, state Republican leaders embezzling

DOI: 10.1057/9781137527813.0006

state funds to play the stock market.[11] However, Tammany's chief leader, Charles Francis "Silent Charlie" Murphy, searches for a more reliable basis for a statewide electoral majority than a chance Republican mishap. After the Democrats' 1910 victory, Murphy, according to Von Drehle, "startled everyone" by appointing "the kindergarten class" or "Tammany Twins" of Robert F. Wagner to be the State Senate leader and Al Smith to lead the Assembly.[12] Wagner and Smith are both under forty, and Murphy wants them to help him formulate a constructive legislative program of social reform that can appeal to the state's new wave of Eastern and Southern European immigrants and women who might soon have the right to vote. "With the installation of Smith and Wagner in the first days of 1911," says Von Drehle, "Charles Murphy promoted the leadership that would move Tammany into an era of change, an era of reform."[13]

In 1912, Tammany ostensibly backs the Fifty-Four-Hour Bill so as to curry favor with new immigrants. However, though Murphy publically supports the bill, he maneuvers to kill it behind the scenes. In 1911, Al Smith feels sorry that Perkins seems to be giving up her summer vacation for nothing. Smith stuns Perkins by telling her that Murphy has ordered Assemblyman Edward Jackson to not let the bill out of his assembly committee. Smith explains Murphy is good friends with the proprietors an owners of Huyler's Candy, and the family vigorously opposes the bill. Murphy will never let the Fifty-Four-Hour Bill pass, Smith tells her, so Perkins should take her previously planned vacation to Europe.[14] However, Perkins continues to work in Albany, and Smith later tells her that this establishes Perkins's credibility with most of the Democratic legislators.[15]

By 1912, Perkins believes she has finally secured enough support to get the bill through the State Senate and the Assembly. However, she is under strict orders from her mentor and boss Florence Kelley and others at the Consumers League to not accept any exemptions to the law. Kelley tells Perkins not to back any bill excluding *any* women from the weekly Fifty-Four-Hour work limit.

The bill's opponents note this "line in the sand" drawn by those leading the Consumers League, the chief lobbying organization fighting to pass the bill. Silent Charlie realizes that his overt obstruction would distance working class voters from Tammany, but believes he can keep his opposition silent by manipulating the Consumers' League's requirements for its support of the Fifty-Four-Hour Bill. Thus, in keeping with his moniker, he can avoid announcing his opposition to the bill and appearing responsible for killing it.

DOI: 10.1057/9781137527813.0006

Both Republicans and Democrats wish to take credit for the bill and thereby increase their appeal to factory workers and immigrants able to vote. However, Murphy has the bill's co-sponsor, Edward D. Jackson, insert a poison pill within the Fifty-Four-Hour Bill. After the bill passes the Senate, it appears likely to also pass the Assembly. Although the Assembly passes the Fifty-Four-Hour Bill, it adds an exemption for women cannery workers. The bill's supporters are pitted against themselves. Since the Consumers League is uncompromising in opposing any exemptions to the bill's maximum hour provision, opponents assume the bill will die and it will look as if the Consumers League had killed it. Tammany could still take credit for supporting the bill.

Because that year's legislative session is concluding, there is no time to reconcile the Senate and the Assembly versions of the bill. Either the Senate accept the lower house's version of the law or it will die for that legislative year. Many progressive senators honor the League's wishes, taking their voting cue from Perkins, the Consumers League representative.

When Perkins learns about the Assembly's maneuver she initially abides by the strict orders of her superiors, Kelley in New York City and Pauline Goldmark in Albany. However, in a last minute change of heart, Perkins decides that she owes it to the overwhelming majority of New York State's working women and children to accept the compromise. In an unusual act of courage Perkins changes her mind and decides to disobey her famed League supervisors. Perkins is especially defiant because Goldmark is present in the Senate and would soon be telling state senators that the League is against the bill as Perkins stands next to her telling the same senators the opposite. Although Perkins is fibbing, m any senators feel a personal connection with Perkins and believe her even though Goldmark is her supervisor.[16]

By reversing herself, Perkins feels she has successfully called the Assembly's bluff. However, State Senator "Big Tim" Sullivan, also called "the King of the Bowery," startles Perkins by taking her into his confidence. Sullivan alerts her to hidden legislative pitfalls designed to keep the Assembly's version of the bill from getting a Senate vote. According to Sullivan, State Senator Robert Wagner, who voted for the bill, is secretly working with Murphy, who after all has been the chief sponsor of Wagner's swift rise within state government. Perkins knows Sullivan's confidential information is correct when Wagner, the Senate's acting chair, does not recognize senators trying to introduce the Assembly's version of the bill for a vote in the Senate.[17]

DOI: 10.1057/9781137527813.0006

Seeing that Perkins feels defeated, Big Tim again confides in her: "Me sister was a poor girl, and she went out to work when she was young. I feel kinda sorry for them poor girls that work the way you say they work. I'd like to do them a good turn. I'd like to do you a good turn. You don't know much about this parliamentary stuff do you?"[18]

Perkins confirms her ignorance. "The bosses thought they was going to kill your bill," say Sullivan, "but they forgot about Tim Sullivan."[19] Schlesinger writes that Big Tim Sullivan "particularly influenced" Perkins by teaching her that "even professional politicians had hearts and could be enlisted in good causes."[20]

Sullivan explains to Perkins that though Wagner had promised to report the bill out of the Senate Rules Committee and onto the Senate floor, Murphy's "plan" is to have the Lieutenant Governor leave the Senate chamber so that Wagner temporarily presides over the State Senate. This causes a conflict of interest, barring Wagner from calling together the Senate Rules Committee and thus preventing the amended Fifty-Four-Hour Bill a Senate floor vote.[21]

Sullivan knows how to counter this tactic. Since Wagner, the presiding officer of the Rules Committee, cannot call the committee to order, Sullivan, the Rules Committee's ranking member, now can. Sullivan shouts, "a report from the Rules Committee!" From the back of the Senate chamber, recalls Perkins, she can see Wagner turn white. Although Wagner calls Sullivan out of order since Wagner is head of the Rules Committee, the Senate parliamentarian rule in Sullivan's favor.[22] Sullivan seems to have succeeded. He introduces the Assembly's version of the bill. The Senate will vote on it.

Democrats do not know what to do. The Senate is in an uproar. Bewildered senators rush to the back of the chamber to ask Perkins, who needs to stay behind the brass railing, if introducing the amended bill is a trick. Should they vote for it? She emphatically answers, "Yes. I'm for it. I've authorized it. We've authorized it. We want it." However, Goldmark stands right next to her telling state senators and Perkins, "No. We don't want it. You mustn't say that."[23]

Adding to the confusion, the state constitution requires the bill to pass with a majority of all the fifty-one New York state senators, more than merely a majority of those present, since the bill is coming out of the Rules Committee and the Assembly. Some state senators already left, and, decisively, Wagner manages to get two senators to change their votes. To everyone's surprise, the amended bill fails to pass: 24–12, although

Wagner and Murphy's senate "lieutenant," State Senator James A. Foley, vote for the amended version.

However, McManus and Perkins realize that since Sullivan has introduced the bill out of the Rules Committee and voted for it, Sullivan can, after the Senate votes to reconsider, reintroduce the bill as an internal Senate matter that would only require a majority of the senators present. Under these circumstances, the bill will definitely pass.[24]

But there is another problem: Tim Sullivan and his cousin, New York State Senator Christy Sullivan, vote (out of order at the start of the roll call) and immediately leave, not anticipating another vote, to catch a boat to New York. Perkins looks at her watch. It is seven-thirty and their "Hudson River steamboat" is scheduled to leave at eight. She speaks on the phone with Sullivan and she manages to have Big Tim and his cousin pulled off the boat. Perkins sends a cab to bring them back to the Capitol building.

Knowing a majority of the senators present will vote for the Fifty-Four-Hour Bill, the bill's opponents think of a new tactic. They ask for a "closed call," meaning that the doors to the Senate will be locked as soon as the senators begin voting for reconsideration. Wagner, again presiding, rules in favor of the closed vote. If Big Tim does not return to reintroduce the bill before the motion to reconsider concludes, he will be shut out of the Senate. The new version of the Fifty-Four-Hour Bill would not reach the Senate floor for a vote and would be legislatively dead for at least a year.

The bill's proponents stage an unusual filibuster to give Tim Sullivan time to reach the Capitol building. Senate rules allow for each senator to speak for five minutes concerning a motion to reconsider. McManus is said to speak "drivel." State Senator Franklin D. Roosevelt, who votes for the bill, lectures about birds for five minutes, although Perkins does not recall FDR's presence or his voting in the affirmative.

Sullivan's health is not good. He is rumored to be suffering from syphilis and a year later a state court determines him to have a debilitating mental illness and commits him to an institution from which he escapes and is subsequently severed in two on a railroad track by an oncoming train. Years later in the White House, Roosevelt recalls Sullivan to Perkins and he sheds tears although Perkins never suspected Roosevelt had any affection for Big Tim. "Big Tim's heart was in the right place," FDR tells Perkins through tears. However, the president acknowledges that Sullivan did not understand the kind of "modern government" in which Perkins and FDR are engaged.[25]

In the last minutes of the final five-minute speech, with only a few minutes remaining before the Senate doors slam on Big Tim, the Sullivan cousins jog into the Senate. Tim is gasping for breath but smiling broadly. After missing the taxi Perkins sent, Big Tim had run up a hill to the Capitol building. He enters the Senate floor just in time shouting, "Record me in the affirmative."

The Fifty-Four-Hour Bill passes 27–16. Pandemonium breaks out in the galleries. Although they vote for the bill, Wagner and Foley sulk. Perkins is jubilant but she expects the Consumers League to fire her when she returns to New York. To her surprise, Kelley congratulates her. In fact, the cannery worker exemption is repealed the next year with little fanfare. Perkins receives a valuable pragmatic lesson.

Perkins's pragmatism breaks ground within the idealistic world of social work, leading her to pioneer social work's intermeshing with government. According to Schlesinger, Perkins is "operating in the area where social work and politics intersect."[26] Like politicians, Perkins values personal contacts. However, she uses her contacts in order to diagnose and address social ills.

Perkins is professionalizing social work in an alternative manner to how social work is then being accepted as a valid profession. By 1917 Mary Ellen Richmond's analysis of individual social casework in *Social Diagnosis* causes Abraham Flexner to reassess social work. He says Richmond transforms social work into a communicable and teachable profession. For Richmond, casework, "effected individual by individual," is social work's professional mode.[27] As formulated by Richmond's 1917 *Social Diagnosis*, individual casework assigns a social worker to an individual or a family. The social worker concentrates on each "case" and how an individual can use all available resources to function better in her or his environment. The caseworker tends to work upon an individual, on a "case-by-case" basis, and not from a more societal view. The newer kind of social workers do not normally concern themselves with larger solutions through their social advocacy.[28]

Before World War I individual social casework begins to overshadow the social reform advocacy that had previously typified social work.

Richmond's casework method facilitates the advent of the social worker as a mental health therapist, and Richmond articulates a need for this turn within social work. World War I accelerates this development. Social worker therapists are needed to treat World War I soldiers suffering from battle fatigue. After the war the mental health therapist role of

DOI: 10.1057/9781137527813.0006

social workers steadily grows. Under the umbrella of individual social casework, government has a manageable and depoliticized manner of employing social workers. New social workers increasingly do not require a progressive mindset.

A correspondence between social work and individual casework, emphasizing social work as a means of resolving personal problems, marginalizes activists within the social work profession. Porter Lee, another innovator in teaching the casework method, says social work was "once a cause" but is now assimilated as "a function of a well-regulated community."[29] With a growing emphasis upon social work's shift toward casework, collective advocacy in social work loses sway.[30] Unreflective of Richmond's aims, social casework reinforces assuming all problems are individual in origin and personal in terms of responsibility rather than social, political, or economic problems.

In the 1920s, for instance, in part responding to Supreme Court rulings against government regulation of child labor, Wiley Swift, the executive secretary of the Child Labor Committee, a social work agency advocating child labor regulation, characterizes this shift in the social work movement: "From now on the movement will be more gradual and necessarily less spectacular."[31] World War I marks a general change in the nature of social workers. Social workers enter the profession after the war lacking the "strong sense of mission" of previous social workers. Social workers are no longer called "settlement workers."[32] Younger social workers no longer live amongst the poor in settlement houses. George Martin links this to a shift from a sense of common cause between social workers and the poor to a new social worker and "client" relationship.[33] "Vital social reforms," says Abraham Epstein, "are left to languish and social workers as a group take but little interest in them."[34]

The new social workers, says Martin, emphasize "casework" and "psychoanalysis instead of social agitation.... They were inclined to concentrate on adjusting individuals to their environment rather than working on social legislation."[35] In direct contrast, Perkins seeks to change societal conditions causing poverty, unlike the younger social workers wishing to help the poor adapt to those conditions.[36] While new social workers tend to find problems within an economically poor individual, Perkins believes poverty is society's problem. For Perkins the society and the individual function together. "It is better that a misfortune falling on an individual should be distributed and borne lightly by the whole

DOI: 10.1057/9781137527813.0006

community," says Perkins, "rather than that the individual should be crushed by the weight of his own misfortune."[37]

Nonetheless, social work as seen through the lens of casework contributes to Perkins's pragmatic social work perspective. She vitalizes a progressive sense of social work at a time when, as Dan Huff observes, "the nation turned away from reform."[38] However, casework can also aid social reform, and Perkins applies the casework method to social and political problems. The "cases" that Perkins processes, however, are often complex social issues, and their treatment requires sensitive group analysis, or "conferencing."

Casework aids Perkins in conceiving of social problems as "cases," opening them up to a consideration of their political dimensions so that long-term solutions can be found. Through this kind of "casework" thinking, she helps redefine the Triangle Fire investigations into a much more widespread "case" of workplace conditions. Through Perkins, it becomes the government's charge to regulate these conditions. Due to Perkins, New York State's Triangle Fire "casework" results in the enactment of revolutionary fire prevention and workplace safety regulations. Perkins utilizes mindsets associated with casework in a manner consistent with the boldness of early social work.

Richmond stresses the caseworker's role as one of connecting the client with resources. However, Perkins addresses societal conditions that impoverish, and Tammany Hall is a key resource in accomplishing this. Perkins's commitment to the "*human* nature of work" provides a bridge to Tammany.[39] Although Tammany politicians can be corrupt and nontransparent in their methods, they can also understand the humanity of those they represent.

Perkins needs to ally with Democratic politicians with whom her fellow social workers would not associate. Many social workers, such as Jane Addams and Florence Kelley, are lifelong Republicans. Tammany politicians are not likely allies. When Perkins admits to being a Democrat at a party, her social work friends boo her, telling her she is befriending "the scum of the earth." Even when she explains that Tammany helps to pass the bills she is "interested in," her friends are horrified by her party affiliation.[40] However, she feels many Tammany politicians are concerned with the "human" dimensions of their working constituents.

In a sense, Perkins extends the Consumers League's agenda to Tammany Hall. Politicians believe working with Perkins increases their popularity. "That the Democratic Party became dominant in New York," says Perkins, is due to Democrats developing "programs for prevention of poverty and for improving the conditions of life."⁴¹ If Perkins needs Tammany legislative know-how to pass the Fifty-Four-Hour Bill, limiting the work hours of women and children, Tammany needs the credibility of Perkins's progressive agenda to gain New York State political dominance.

A few years after the Fifty-Four-Hour Bill vote, Perkins goes to Tammany Hall on Fourteenth Street to ask Charles F. Murphy for his support to pass factory building code legislation. He asks her, "You are the young lady, aren't you, who managed to get the Fifty-Four-Hour bill passed? Well, young lady I opposed that plan.... It is my observation that the bill made us many votes. I will tell all the boys to give all the help they can to this new bill."⁴²

It helps Tammany that its leaders grew up within the poor or working classes so they could see the virtues of Perkins's social work goals. Perkins's ideas give the politicians persuasive rigor. At Alfred E. Smith's funeral, Perkins hears a former Tammany leader ask another where Smith got his progressive ideals. "He read a book," says the politician. "He knew Frances Perkins and she is a book."⁴³

This anecdote does not tell the entire story because Smith sees the political potential in Perkins and wants to help her for his own purposes. To make the most of this opportunity, Perkins devises a tactic utilizing social work's growing focus on casework. In the service of new modes of government and social work now joining forces, Perkins, who starts her career in the more women-centered world of social work, consciously considers how to elicit the help of hardened yet often well-meaning male politicians.

Notes

1   Martin, p. 98.
2   Perkins, *Roosevelt*, p. 14.
3   Columbia University Libraries, Part 1, p. 86.
4   Ibid., p. 87.
5   Ibid.
6   Ibid.
7   Ibid., pp. 28–29.

DOI: 10.1057/9781137527813.0006

8   Ibid., p. 41.
9   Arthur M. Schlesinger, Jr., *The Age Of Roosevelt, Volume III, 1935–1936: The Politics of Upheaval* (Boston: Houghton Mifflin Company, 1960), pp. 646, 649.
10   Ibid., p. 81.
11   Ibid., p. 200.
12   Von Drehle, p. 200.
13   Ibid., p. 201.
14   Ibid., p. 206.
15   Martin, p. 81.
16   Ibid., pp. 96–97.
17   Ibid., p. 96.
18   Coleman, p. 28.
19   Martin, p. 97.
20   Schlesinger, vol. II, p. 299.
21   Martin, p. 95.
22   Ibid., p. 96.
23   Ibid.
24   Ibid., p. 97.
25   Perkins, *Roosevelt*.
26   Schlesinger, vol. II, p. 299.
27   Arthur E. Fink, Everett E. Wilson, and Merrill B. Conover, *The Field of Social Work* (New York: Holt, Rhienhart, and Winston, 1964), p. 76.
28   Martin, pp. 193–194.
29   The Profession of Social Work & The International Federation of Social Workers, "Social Work: A Definition—2000," *The Social Welfare History Project*, http://www.socialwelfarehistory.com/programs/social-work-a-definition-2000/ (accessed June 1, 2013).
30   Ibid.
31   Clark A. Chambers, *A Seedtime of Reform, American Social Service and Social Action, 1918–1933* (Minneapolis: University of Minnesota Press, 1963), p. 46.
32   Martin, p. 192.
33   Ibid., p. 193.
34   Epstein, p. 100.
35   Martin, p. 193.
36   Ibid., p. 194.
37   Frances Perkins, "Social Security Here and Abroad," *Foreign Affairs*, 13:3 (April, 1935): 374.
38   Dan Huff, http://web1.boisestate.edu/SOCWORK/DHUFF/history/chapts/4-2b.htm.
39   Newman, p. 84.
40   Downey, p. 43.
41   Perkins, *Roosevelt*, p. 17.

DOI: 10.1057/9781137527813.0006

42   Martin, p. 99.

43   Matthew Josephson and Hannah Josephson, *Al Smith, Hero of the Cities: A Political Portrait Drawing on the Papers of Frances Perkins* (Boston: Houghton Mifflin Company, 1969) p. 102.

DOI: 10.1057/9781137527813.0006

4
The Perkins Persona

Abstract: *In the 1910s, social work recasts itself. While this leads to depoliticizing casework, it also individualizes it and opens it to psychological methodology. Perkins uses this psychological dimension for political ends. Perkins's experience with State Senator Frawley opens her eyes to the way psychological transference can further her political aims. Her experience as a social worker enables her to apply casework to her male peers and to the working of government itself.*

Keywords: casework; friendly visitors; James Frawley; Mary Ellen Richmond; psychoanalytic method; social work; William Sulzer

Miller, Stephen Paul. *The New Deal as a Triumph of Social Work: Frances Perkins and the Confluence of Early Twentieth Century Social Work with Mid-Twentieth Century Politics and Government.* New York: Palgrave Macmillan, 2016. DOI: 10.1057/9781137527813.0007.

DOI: 10.1057/9781137527813.0007

In the 1910s, social workers increasingly view themselves as caseworkers. They thus utilize psychological and psychoanalytic methods. In one such method, the patient unconsciously sees the therapist as a parent, and the therapist, who may now be a social worker, intelligently uses this psychological transference of the parent onto the therapist to make the patient conscious of her or his unconscious drives and inhibitions. This Freudian method is termed "transference." Of course, Perkins does not use transference as an analyst would. However, she knowingly, if informally, uses something like transference to draw politicians into trusting her with pertinent and confidential information.

Mary Ellen Richmond characterizes the caseworker as one who engenders confidence and communication. Richmond stresses the importance of a caseworker's "flexible focus," a focus that is more cognizant of interpersonal interactions than the average government administrator. As a lobbyist in Albany, Perkins becomes aware of her ability to enter into professional yet personal relationships with politicians.

One incident shows Perkins how she work within a political environment she experiences as "full of emotion.[1] In 1913, State Senator James J. Frawley chairs a committee accusing Governor William Sulzer of misusing campaign contributions. Sulzer provokes Tammany leadership by "seeking to pursue an agenda of good government reforms." Sultzer does not recognize Tammany's patronage system. Tammany thus goes after Sultzer for his fiscal indescretions by launching a legislative investigative committee[2] resulting in his impeachment and removal from office. The weight of impeachment, recalls Perkins, hangs heavily on everyone in the state legislature. When a behind-closed-door compromise with Frawley cannot be reached, "They almost had nervous breakdowns. They just couldn't bear what they had launched," Perkins remembers.[3]

Perkins does not know Frawley well. "Nobody thought Frawley had good qualities. He is rough," says Perkins. "When he rose to speak he was very ungrammatical."[4] However, when Perkins encounters Frawley in August 1913 in the Albany State Capitol building, Frawley feels he knows her. When she simply says, "Good afternoon, Senator" to Frawley, says Perkins: "He took a kind of gasp as though I was a ghost out of a book.... He grabbed me by the hand, he wrung it and he began to sort of gasp and said, 'Oh, Miss Perkins. We've done a terrible thing!...Oohh we're in a dreadful predicament.' He pulled his handkerchief out. He began to mop his face and then began to sob into his handkerchief, holding onto my hand all the time."[5]

DOI: 10.1057/9781137527813.0007

Perkins is stunned that Frawley confides details about Tammany's secret failed negotiations with Sulzer. She commiserates with him but, "He carried on frightfully and then he burst into a great sob as I was saying, 'I'm so sorry. I'm sure it's hard for you. I'm sure it's hard for the governor.' I was saying nothings, just to say something sympathetic."[6] At this point Frawley crystallizes the experience for Perkins: "[Frawley] said with this great sob, as though to justify his tears and his complete emotional collapse, 'Every man's got a mother, you know.' "[7] In an interesting twist upon "casework," Perkins adds that Frawley "wasn't a real case." In other words, he does not need a mental health care social caseworker. Perkins continues, "He was just a typical male," meaning that he is rather a case study for the much broader subject of "typical males," providing insight into how a woman might work with men in government so as to facilitate good government through social work.[8]

Frawley's remark that "Every man's got a mother" resonates in Perkins's mind. "I never forgot that. That is the beginning of a great deal of wisdom on my part. I pondered over this remark. At first I thought it was funny," says Perkins. "I told it to one or two intimates as funny and they thought it was funny." However, Perkins soon realizes that this is not a laughing matter. It is "significant" that Frawley trusts her and she wants to cultivate that kind of trust. She believes that Frawley speaks to her out of the blue not only because she is a woman but also because he thinks of her "as a good woman [who] wouldn't go around making sport of him...he really didn't think this. It was all subconscious. I never told the story for a joke after I realized that."[9]

Perkins might not think of herself as a caseworker or a therapist. However, she is certainly familiar with casework, and she understands how therapeutic casework might "transfer" a parent–child relationship into a therapist–patient relationship. Perkins concludes "that the way men take women in political life is to associate them with motherhood." She decides to use this association since it seems to be a "primitive and primary attitude" for "ninety-nine percent" of men to "know and respect" their mothers.[10] Perkins becomes "sure" that she has come upon "the way to get things done." Through this kind of transference, she believes she has found a pragmatic amalgam of social casework and politics.[11]

It is interesting in this respect that William James associates pragmatism with a seemingly feminine quality of integrating and moving beyond rigid positions. Emphasizing a particular aspect of being a woman, Perkins decides to "behave" and "dress and...comport [her]

DOI: 10.1057/9781137527813.0007

self [to] remind [male politicians] subconsciously of their mothers." She takes seriously how Frawley assumes he can trust and freely share his thoughts and emotions with her. Because of this experience Perkins changes her "whole approach." She begins wearing a "black dress with the bow of white at the throat as a kind of official uniform."[12] Reflecting Perkins's preference for empirical research, she diligently recorded how "it has always worked" for her in the political world.

"Frances Perkins," Schlesinger notes, "later recalled how some of the most powerful [American businessmen] like Alfred Sloan of General Motors, unmanned by the dangerous fact that the Secretary of Labor was a woman, poured into her ears long, tormented confessionals to justify careers which, for a moment, baffled even the men themselves."[13] Perkins has no doubts about the effectiveness of the motherly persona she perfects. "I've had so many demonstrations," claims Perkins. "I've got a big red envelope full of episodes of that sort which have indicated to me that that's how they took women."[14] Indeed, FDR later uses Perkins's empathetic skills by regularly asking her to soothe slighted cabinet members.

According to Richmond, empathy is the social worker's key skill. For example, only by treating the poor as individuals, each with characteristics as unique as those of the rich, is it possible to "recognize them" and facilitate their "sturdy self-reliance and independence."[15] Richmond stresses the importance of the social worker's frame of mind, asserting that the social worker "must rid himself, first of all, of the conventional picture of the poor."[16] "Our relations with our poor friends must be as natural as possible."[17] The slightest communicative nuance can be crucial: "Indirect suggestion is powerful."[18] In other words, the state of mind and sensitivity with which the social worker approaches her or his task is of paramount importance. The social worker must be mentally "flexible."[19] "Rules save the trouble of thinking, but a more flexible method is to let the order of seeing 'outside sources' grow naturally."[20] The mindset of being guided by a more "flexible method" than mere "rules" describes Perkins's bending of the Consumers League rules to pass the Fifty-Four-Hour bill and the ease with which Perkins allies herself with politicians whom she knows are "undoubtedly corrupt," such as Thomas McManus.

Perkins is a kind of nineteenth century "friendly visitor" to the world of politics. In *Friendly Visiting among the Poor: A Handbook for Charity Workers*, Richmond uses the "friendly visitor" who "improve[s]" the poor's "condition permanently" as a model for the typical social worker.[21]

DOI: 10.1057/9781137527813.0007

Indeed something like individual casework has long been associated with social work. Casework has roots in the nineteenth century practice of individual volunteers from charity organizations paying friendly visits to those in need. It is thus not surprising that Richmond's 1903 book *Friendly Visiting among the Poor* is an important precursor to Richmond's *Social Diagnosis*, which establishes casework as a means of professionalizing social work. Many of the sentiments expressed in *Friendly Visiting among the Poor* remind us that Richmond's caseworker model is instrumental in social work becoming the main provider of mental health care in the United States.

Richmond's description of casework emphasizes the caseworker's perspective. While this may not be tantamount to stressing psychologically analytical processes, Richmond sounds a little like Freud when she compares a medical doctor's comments concerning the symptoms of a disease to those of a social problem. "They are generally presented to us *from an angle*, and with one symptom, generally a misleading one, in foreground. From this point of view we must reason ourselves back into the deeper processes and more obscure causes which guide our therapeutic endeavor."[22]

Perkins often speaks of the need for government to act as a kind of facilitator, psychologist or teacher. For instance, as the head of the New York State Industrial Commission, she says the government must "become the clearing house for information on the techniques of industrial welfare and human relations" so that "industrial law develops from the inside out" because: "as the psychologists say, [law] is first 'inwardly realized,' follow[ing] the same pattern as all nature and is harmoniously and successfully expressed in reasoned action…. A law which rests on the consent of the governed is always secure. It is, therefore, always worth the time and energy it takes for government officials to reason it out, even with the most obtuse and recalcitrant employer."[23]

It is perhaps relevant that Perkins's husband is mentally ill. Her encounter with Frawley occurs in August 1913 and she marries Paul Wilson in September 1913. Although she is not forced to consider the depths of her husband's bipolar illness until 1918, she is already aware of mental health therapy. Concerning her husband's illness, she says that she manages to avoid a "Freudian collapse" herself.[24] It is also possible that she may have attributed retrospective significance to the incident with Frawley, assimilating what she might have learned from for her husband's treatment. Whatever the case, Perkins is a social worker who

DOI: 10.1057/9781137527813.0007

works in a professional world with increasing numbers of caseworkers, and it makes sense to consider her within this context to understand how she uses casework for social reform.

In a sense Perkins's two most celebrated "cases" are Social Security and the Triangle Shirtwaist Factory fire. Perkins, with Al Smith's help, manages to open this case of the Triangle Fire to a plethora of other dangerous and unhealthy workplace conditions for the New York State Factory Investigating Commission to explore. Tammany Hall thus gives Perkins a grand platform to show her conference method to government officials and the public.

Notes

1   Columbia University Libraries, Part 1, p. 223.
2   Downey, p. 44.
3   Columbia University Libraries, Part 1, p. 229.
4   Ibid., p. 228.
5   Ibid., pp. 229–230.
6   Ibid.
7   Ibid., p. 231.
8   Ibid.
9   Ibid.
10   Ibid.
11   Ibid., pp. 231–232.
12   Ibid.
13   Schlesinger, Vol. III, p. 424.
14   Columbia University Libraries, Part 1, p. 232.
15   Mary E. Richmond, *Friendly Visiting among the Poor: A Handbook for Charity Workers* (New York: Macmillan, 1903), p. 9.
16   Ibid., p. 10.
17   Ibid., p. 66.
18   Ibid., p. 77.
19   Mary E. Richmond, *Social Diagnosis* (New York: Russell Sage Foundation, 1919), p. 8.
20   Ibid., p. 147.
21   Richmond, *Friendly*, p. v.
22   Ibid., p. 352.
23   Perkins, "Helping," p. 626.
24   Martin, p. 136.

DOI: 10.1057/9781137527813.0007

5
Enter Populists. Enter Progressives. Enter Social Workers. Enter Frances Perkins

Abstract: *This chapter contextualizes the progressives' role in shaping social work, dating back to America's founding. The Constitutional framers implicitly anticipate economic rights. However, Perkins and FDR must draw our their implications so as to account for an American antipathy towards targeted rights.*

Keywords: Frances Perkins; Fourteenth Amendment; individual rights; Rights-based; social work

Miller, Stephen Paul. *The New Deal as a Triumph of Social Work: Frances Perkins and the Confluence of Early Twentieth Century Social Work with Mid-Twentieth Century Politics and Government.* New York: Palgrave Macmillan, 2016. DOI: 10.1057/9781137527813.0008.

DOI: 10.1057/9781137527813.0008

Early American social workers distinguish themselves from other turn of the century progressives by directly engaging themselves with the poor. However, social work springs from America's progressive movements. Frances Perkins attests to this by describing how, as a young woman, falling under the Progressive Era's spell leads her to a life of social work. However, few if any progressive thinkers articulate a constitutional rationale for mandating the government to ameliorate poverty. Emphasizing the importance social work assigns to assisting the poor, and transferring that responsibility to government, might equip social workers and likeminded Americans with a conceptual basis for establishing the validity of economic rights within an American constitutional system.

However, the Great Depression calls for exercising economic rights that are already implicit within early American social work's aims. Social work provides theoretical context and an experiential frame of reference for ideas about "unalienable" nature of economic rights. In this manner, social work profoundly alters and adds explicitly and contextually to the "progressive" American mindset. Tellingly, the lone group of surviving early twentieth century progressives that grow into core FDR backers is composed of those who either had worked as early social workers or had been associated with social work. In fact, many if not most turn of the century American progressives who live long enough to experience the Great Depression resist the New Deal.

What accounts for early progressives not initially joining the New Deal? This concerns concepts informing the American republic from its birth, concepts presupposing individually inherent rights, rights that are first conceived to protect individuals from the government. This relatively "negative" presupposition of rights as it relates to government clashes with the theoretical underpinnings of government as a "positive" agent or facilitator of business, finance, commerce, agriculture, and manufacturing infrastructure.

One reason that the original framers of the Constitution do not expound upon economic rights is that rights are in large part viewed as the earlier Declaration describes them—"truths" that are "self-evident." From a twenty-first century perspective this might appear to draw upon naïve faith in a pre-existing human, theological, or natural order. However, in the late eighteenth century, the founders emphasize it is the superior rights of monarchs and aristocrats that are not "self-evident." Aristocracy, rather, is an imposed construction.

DOI: 10.1057/9781137527813.0008

Garry Wills's *Inventing America* also reminds us that in the eighteenth century imagination rights are linked with responsibilities so that asserting the rights of everyone implies one's own, and not the king's, responsibility and self-determination.[1]

Frances Perkins's manner of social work presupposes economic rights as safeguards against poverty. Do Perkins's ideas fit within America's tradition of conceptualizing rights? Yes, but there are structural problems. Eighteenth century concieve rights in the negative sense of protecting something already present within individuals. However, the founders must also frame a positive constitutional infrastructure facilitating public interactions within business, finance, manufacturing, and the economics of agriculture. Because private rights mix poorly with the collective structuring of an environment that can sustain the nation's economic life, it is difficult to get at the heart of individual economic rights. It is difficult to guarantee a minimal, or prosperous, level of economic livelihood as a positive "right." The founders primarily concern themselves with setting up a structure allowing government to act positively to promote what we might term "collective economic rights" to do business and defend this livelihood. Although prosperous, property- holding white males lead early America, the Constitution opposes aristocracy and the exclusivity of any particular group. The Constitution guarantees economic rights only within the context of an early American abundance of land and resources. In a sense, the Constitution is intended positively to assist the functioning of impersonal economic units. The Constitution does not create a government meant to identify and assist individuals, whether those individuals are disadvantaged or not.

The founders do not entertain the framing of individual economic rights in part because they do not envision the need for them. Two questions about the unamended Constitution bear upon this. Is the Constitution based upon or relevant to any notion of rights? If so, do such rights address poverty? Obviously, "unalienable rights" underlie the Declaration of Independence's "causes which impel the [colonies] to the separation." However, it is often assumed that the Constitution does not in any way tackle "rights" until the Bill of Rights amendments are ratified.

And of course the urgency propelling the framers of the Constitution is economic. They must establish a legal "infrastructure" that will sustain the economy. Intriguingly, the sole time the word "right" is used in the original Constitution is in Article I, section 8, which enumerates

DOI: 10.1057/9781137527813.0008

what "the Congress shall have Power To" do. Among such items as the power to "lay and collect Taxes, Duties, Imposts and Excises, to pay the Debts and provide for the common Defence and general Welfare of the United States," "borrow Money on the credit of the United States," "regulate Commerce with foreign Nations," "establish an uniform Rule of Naturalization, and uniform Laws on the subject of Bankruptcies," "coin Money," "establish Post Offices and post Roads," "declare War," "raise and support Armies" and a "Navy," is Congress's power "To promote the Progress of Science and useful Arts, by securing for limited Times to Authors and Inventors the exclusive *Right* to their respective Writings and Discoveries" (italics added). The unamended Constitution only mentions "right" in the sense of a "copyright," as an intellectual property. This Constitutional right, known as the "copyright clause," is lacking within the Articles of Confederation.

The use of the word "right" in this clause is telling because it applies to individual "Authors and Inventors." These individuals have "exclusive Right[s]" related to the supposition of their ownership of their "Writings and Discoveries," of, that is, their properties. Two related points are of interest. First, "rights" are mentioned here because a right is suspect if it does not apply to an individual, albeit, to any individual.

Second, however, the Constitution's framers realize the legal fiction implicit in their articulation of "copy*right*" as an individual right. After all, corporations, especially ones connected with the English monarchy, own properties such as copyrights. For purposes of contract in particular, English common law holds that corporations are legally fictive individuals. The Marshall Court's 1819 *Dartmouth v. Woodward* ruling upholds this understanding of corporations as people in the prescribed sense of being able to enter into valid contracts. This ruling is quite understandable since corporations cannot otherwise agree to contracts, and, in 1819, there is consensus among Americans that corporate ventures are vital for national development.

Why does the Constitution not mention corporations? When the Constitution is written corporations are chiefly linked to crown and church. Curbs upon these kinds of corporations are implicitly included in the Constitution when, for instance, the final clause of Article I, section 9 states, "No Title of Nobility shall be granted by the United States: And no Person holding any Office of Profit or Trust under them, shall, without the Consent of the Congress, accept of any present, Emolument, Office, or Title, of any kind whatever, from any King, Prince, or foreign State."

DOI: 10.1057/9781137527813.0008

Framers such as Alexander Hamilton contend these kinds of curbs in conjunction with the extensive working of constitutional checks and balances make moot the inclusion of a "bill of rights." In fact, Republican-Democrats such as James Madison agree with Hamilton. Even when Madison changes his opinion about the importance of drafting a "bill of rights," he still largely agrees with Hamilton since Madison tells Thomas Jefferson that he thinks the significance of a constitutional bill of rights lies primarily in clarifying and amplifying for the American people what the Constitution has already substantially accomplished. Indeed, when Madison proposes the Bill of Rights he says it is "limited to points which are important in the eyes of many and can be objectionable in those of none. *The structure & stamina of Govt. are as little touched as possible*" (italics added).

How can Madison take this view? How does the original Constitution protect fundamental individual rights? Hamilton notes significant protections such as: "Article I, section 3, clause 7, 'Judgment in cases of impeachment shall not extend further than to removal from office, but the party convicted shall nevertheless be liable and subject to indictment, trial, judgment and punishment, according to law'; section 9 of the same article, clause 2, 'The privilege of the writ of *habeas corpus* shall not be suspended, unless...the public safety may require it'; Clause 3, 'No bill of attainder or *ex post facto* law shall be passed'; clause 8, 'No title of nobility shall be granted by the United States...'; Article III, section 2, clause 3, 'The trial of all crimes, except in cases of impeachment, shall be by jury...'; section 3, of the same article, '...No person shall be convicted of treason unless on the testimony of two witnesses to the same overt act, or on confession in open court; and clause 2, of the same section, '...no attainder of treason shall work corruption of blood, or forfeiture, except during the life of the person attainted.'" Hamilton lists many other existing Constitutional protections. "Averting therefore to the substantial meaning of a bill of rights," says Hamilton, "it is absurd to allege that it is not to be found in the work of the convention." He argues that many of the rights in the proposed Bill of Rights are already enshrined in English common law. Hamilton also points out the rights protected in Article IV, section 2: "The Citizens of each State shall be entitled to all Privileges and Immunities of Citizens in the several States." Most significantly, this article has been used to recognize the legality of a gay marriage performed in another state.

Although ten of Madison's twelve proposed amendments are soon ratified, there is little agreement about how practicable the individual

DOI: 10.1057/9781137527813.0008

rights protection implicit in the first eight amendments will be. It is not until the twentieth century that the incorporation principle is read into the Fourteenth Amendment, and the Bill of Rights becomes active on a national basis and comes into play in many of the Warren Court's monumental decisions. Of course, in the last third of the nineteenth century, private corporate interests prevail upon these Fourteenth Amendments "equal protection" rights. In effect, the Supreme Court extends corporate rights of contract to individual rights. This is indicative of a loss of the productive manner of cooperation between government and business for the common good that is generally assumed in early America.

Progressive and populist movements attempt to restore something like this previous American consensus. Perkins and Roosevelt each in their own way are crucial in articulating how Jeffersonian "rights" can be conceptualized to make American progressivism work after World War I. After all, as Cass R. Sunstein says, "Constitutions written before 1900 are unlikely to contain anything like the second bill" of economic rights.[2]

Late nineteenth century progressivism and populism address the group interests of workers, farmers, and small business owners who are dominated by post-Civil War corporate capitalism. However, populists and progressives do not fight to extend the Enlightenment rights upon which the United States is founded into an economic realm. Instead, they see the nation's problems emanating from large, undemocratic, and, as William R. Brock puts it, "malign controlling interest[s] behind politics."[3]

This has been the prevailing view until recent decades when several historians argue that turn of the century populists are more enlightened than previously thought. In fact, the populist programs of currency reform favoring rural and small business lenders, more democratic opportunities for political participation, the direct election of US senators, instituting a progressive federal income tax to replace funding the federal government primarily through tariffs on imports that seem to increase the cost of living for small farmers, and public control of railroads are innovative. Indeed, populism informs progressive and New Deal ideas and accomplishments, such as the Tennessee Valley Association's public control of electricity and its infrastructure.

However, many populists primarily want to remove the specter of "Wall Street" so as to reestablish their notions of a Jeffersonian America composed of smaller economic units. Although the populist desire to

DOI: 10.1057/9781137527813.0008

rein in and tax demonized and "alien" financial and industrial forces, and indeed to seize ownership of industries such as railroads from these forces, are themselves significant ideas, most populists arguably wish to return the economy to a recognizable capitalist economic model. They are nostalgic for the pre-industrial world of their parents and grandparents. Brock points out the irony of later European socialists adopting the "terminology that was formulated" by American populists while "the heirs of populism have adapted a conservative pride in capitalist institutions." How is it that these "heirs" now form a large part of the current conservative Republican base? The answer might be embedded in the regional nature of turn of the twentieth century populism. The ingenuity of many of their economic ideas aside, many populists aim to restore effective regional and local control. "The truth is that populist attack on Capitalism (and that of some progressives) was always discriminating; it was never 'capitalists' but always 'some capitalists' who were at fault; the enemy was not the hard-working small businessman of the West, whose prospects were identified with his region, but remote capitalists who manipulated without being aware of local needs," says Brock. "John Pierpont Morgan was the villain, not the Babbits of Main Street. The attack was ethical, concentrated on the immorality of individuals, and did not assume that men were made immoral by the economic system they served."

One might expect to find a deeply grounded aspiration for local and regional control within an area of the nation in which agriculture has always been dominant. This expectation may go far in answering the question in Thomas Frank's 2004 book title, *What's the Matter with Kansas? How Conservatives Won the Heart of America.*

Among the ideological sleight of hand luring working class Kansans to vote Republican is the Republican evocation of the ideological populist mindset fending off the far-off Washington and New York "ruling classes."

Similarly, the progressive movement makes strides in trust busting, industry regulation, and, through constitutional amendments, women's suffrage, the constitutional facilitation of a progressive federal income tax, and the direct popular election of US senators. However, the progressives also chiefly desire a normative if scaled down capitalist societal order. Even an early progressive such as Henry George, who in his widely popular 1879 *Poverty and Progress* identifies the gross economic inequities of the Gilded Age so as to attribute them to the Industrial Revolution

DOI: 10.1057/9781137527813.0008

and its robber barons, remains a relatively conventional free enterprise capitalist whose key remedy for his age's dilemma involves implementing "land" or real estate taxes. The more radical and wholeheartedly socialist 1887 *Looking Backwards* by Edward Bellamy directly figures more into populist than progressive politics, indicating that populists are more fully committed to change than progressives.

Both populists and progressives stop at conceptual roadblocks between political and economic rights. They do not attempt to fold economic rights into political rights so that "Every man has a right to life; and this means that he has also a *right* to make a comfortable living" (italics added), as FDR puts it in his 1932 Commonwealth Club address in San Francisco. In effect, the social work that Frances Perkins previously promotes sets the stage for the formulation of economic rights within New York State and the federal government.

Perkins herself initially articulates to FDR in 1932 and later the American electorate in 1936 how the accomplishments of the administration cannot be understood properly without recognition of economic and social rights. It is difficult for us now to grasp what seems so eye opening about Perkins's summation of what the first FDR administration has done. She startles political operatives by saying, "The Democratic Party has established the idea that the welfare of the people is the first charge upon the government."[4] Why is this statement surprising?

In the United States, "rights" are thought to apply to individuals. Group rights appear un-American because they seemingly create groups that can exercise something like aristocratic prerogatives so that some groups are privileged over others. The very appearance of group rights is problematic for Americans. To present an example that has been at issue since the 1970s, although affirmative action might be justified b y Fourteenth Amendment motives of "equal protection" fostering and protecting individual rights for all, the policy's apparent evocation of set group identities, even if minority identities, makes affirmative action easy prey to opponents framing the benefits of affirmative action as something like group rights. For better or worse, most Americans instinctively suspect any hint of group rights. Works such as Sheryll Cashin's *Place, Not Race: A New Vision of Opportunity in America* (2014) acknowledge the practical effects of race-based affirmative action but attempts to "de-faction" it by basing affirmative action on income and place, paradoxically extending affirmative action to majority identities.

DOI: 10.1057/9781137527813.0008

Ironically, a Supreme Court justice such as Clarence Thomas uses the Fourteenth Amendment's last clause—the "equal protection" clause originally written so as to safeguard the rights of freed slaves—to constitutionally invalidate affirmative action. The Fourteenth Amendment's framers themselves contradict Thomas's reasoning by sponsoring state and local "affirmative action" programs that are large parts of post-Civil War Southern Reconstruction. Nonetheless, it is possible that the very possibility of interpreting affirmative action as a tool of "group rights" alienates the topic of minority rights for many otherwise well-meaning Americans, and affirmative action certainly makes itself a relatively easy target for those who are consciously or unconsciously prejudiced against minorities.

Sensitivity toward what constitutes a "right" is grounded within American character. "The United States was founded on the proclamation of 'unalienable' rights," says Arthur M. Schlesinger, Jr., "and human rights ever since have had a peculiar resonance in the American mind." If these rights do not apply to all individuals they seem to privilege a particular group of individuals. However, group rights reside in protecting the "inalienable rights" of all individuals. If a group right applies to all, it is not strictly speaking a group right, but rather a universal right. Group rights that explicitly are not universal and differentiate among groups and individuals are difficult to sustain in America. For Americans, group rights seemingly diminish the rights of some groups in favor of those of others.

According to the Declaration of Independence, "these United Colonies are, and of *Right* ought to be Free and Independent States" (italics added).

However, the Declaration of Independence asserts a national "group right" since "the King of Great Britain" has not "secure[d]" "certain unalienable Rights" for which "Governments are instituted among Men, deriving their just powers from the consent of the governed,—That whenever any Form of Government becomes destructive of these ends, it is the Right of the People to alter or to abolish it, and to institute new Government." The King's violations of the individual rights of virtually all of his American subjects is said to give the American colonies something resembling a group right to revolt, or in any case a right to join other revolutionaries seeking to regain their ability to exercise their natural rights.

The Declaration of Independence voices the most significant assertion of an American group right until the 1888 *Pembina Consolidated Silver Mining Co. v. Pennsylvania* United States Supreme Court decision.

DOI: 10.1057/9781137527813.0008

However, even when the Supreme Court grants private corporations several significant constitutional "rights," such as the "due process" and "equal protection" rights of the Fourteenth Amendment which are initially intended to safeguard the rights of freed slaves, in addition to the "right of association" of the First Amendment, the court accomplishes this by ruling that a corporation is in certain senses an individual person.

The American judiciary thus plays with a tacitly accepted theoretical line between individual rights and classically theorized economic units. "The eighteenth century political theorists had in mind as the unit of power the individual citizen, and the classic economists had in mind the small firm," observes C. Wright Mills.[5] The *Pembina Consolidated Silver Mining Co. v. Pennsylvania* decision reflects the imbalance that overtakes the United States during the post-Civil War Gilded Age when large corporations can at times in effect buy many of the nation's politicians and judges. In the latter third of the nineteenth century America's inequality of wealth reaches previously "un-American" levels. The *Pembina Consolidated* decision is emblematic of the tyranny of group rights that many Americans instinctively feel. Indeed, the populist and progressive movements manifest within this context. An echo of this can be detected in the 2012 presidential election when Romney is ridiculed for saying, "Corporations are people too, my friend," and in opposition to the Supreme Court's 2010 *Citizens United* decision overruling curbs on corporate funding of election campaigns, curbs dating back to Theodore Roosevelt's presidency. A populist mindset challenges the "rights" of large private corporations to dominate the public realm by using the Fourteenth Amendment to usurp rather than, as the amendment's framers intend, guarantee constitutional human rights.

A social worker such as Frances Perkins strives to reverse the logic implicit in the *Pembina Consolidated* decision. If the Supreme Court gives individual rights to corporations, Perkins sees no problem in giving economic rights to individuals. After all, Jefferson's Declaration says that by "secur[ing] unalienable Rights" government "effect[s]" the "Safety and Happiness" for the individuals "consent[ing]" to be "governed" by it. How can the destitution Perkins sees in the wake of the Industrial Revolution be reconciled with the Declaration of Independence?

Perkins's social work provides a ground to apply "default" Enlightenment rights to the economic livelihoods of individuals and families. FDR also attempts to merge rights and responsibilities. For example, in a famous 1941 remark to Treasury appointee Luther Gulick, Roosevelt explains

DOI: 10.1057/9781137527813.0008

his strategy for making Americans feel that they have a "right" to social security. Gulick suggests to the president that it had been a mistake to levy the social security payroll tax in the mid-1930s when it might have been economically more important to keep the currency in circulation. "I guess you're right on the economics," says FDR: "[The payroll taxes] are politics all the way through. We put those pay roll contributions there so as to give the contributors a legal, moral, and political right to collect their pensions and their unemployment benefits. With those taxes in there, no damn politician can ever scrap my social security program. Those taxes aren't a matter of economics, they're straight politics."[6] For Roosevelt, the Social Security payroll taxes destroy the relief attitude, making Social Security feel like a right. Within this context, the Roosevelt administration makes the important innovation of payroll taxes. This allows government to provide social security before workers claim narrow, "isolated" ownership of their perceived income. This both simplifies tax collection and concretizes the notion of the collective economic sphere that government infrastructure makes possible.

It is important to note that the economic and political domination of private corporations begins only after the Civil War. A century and a half ago the concept that the private economic sphere is one that should work toward the greater public good is still recalled by many as the original "American System," as Henry Clay in 1816 describes a Hamiltonian mode of cooperation between government and business that Jefferson tacitly endorses as president.[7] In fact, a central component of Clay's American System is the construction of the national infrastructure proposed by Jefferson's Treasury Secretary, Albert Gallatin, but delayed by the War of 1812.

The New Deal therefore stresses the American republic's earliest economic consensus, a consensus that despite prevailing post-Civil War ideology always remains at play. The officially mixed private and public economy that the New Deal appears to inaugurate is in fact America's earliest economic model. " 'Mixed' enterprise was the customary organization for important innovations," says Robert A. Lively about the early United States economy, "and government everywhere undertook the role put on it by the people, that of planner, promoter, investor, and regulator." At the turn of the twentieth century, progressive and populist mindsets park to this American political and economic tradition.

Late nineteenth century social workers address urban poverty, and this makes them groundbreaking on several fronts. Most Americans

DOI: 10.1057/9781137527813.0008

then do not acknowledge poverty as a systemic problem. Middle class Americans are often unfamiliar with the working poor, disabled, and chronically unemployed "byproducts" of industrialization. Perkins's middle class family in Massachusetts cannot, says Perkins later, imagine poverty as a problem that in any manner concerns society as a whole or the government.

Perhaps an even greater hurdle involves extending the Enlightenment rights upon which the United States is founded into an economic realm. Progressives and call upon government to check overwhelming economic powers. However, most progressives and populists remain apprehensive about the power of government itself. They are rarely enthusiastic about the federal government acting in a more positive fashion for the greater good. And yet advocating for the poor calls for "assertive government," as Arthur M. Schlesinger, Jr. coins it.

Ironically, at about the time of World War I when social work is being professionalized and depoliticized, pioneering pre-war social workers such as Frances Perkins work with politicians such as Al Smith and Franklin Roosevelt to "professionalize" social work in a different way through government administrative policy. Also ironically, pre-Civil War economic assumptions underlie reformist mindsets of populists, progressives, and social workers.

Notes

1   Garry Wills, *Inventing America: Jefferson's Declaration of Independence* (Boston, MA: Houghton Mifflin Harcourt, 2002). Print.
2   Cass R. Sunstein, *The Second Bill of Rights: FDR's Unfinished Revolution and Why We Need It More Than Ever* (New York: Basic Books, 2004), p. 109.
3   William R. Brock, *The Evolution of American Democracy* (New York: The Dial Press, 1970), pp. 204–205.
4   Columbia University Libraries, Part 7, pp. 11–14.
5   C. Wright Mills, *Power Elite* (New York: Oxford University Press, 1999), p. 266.
6   http://www.archives.gov/exhibits/treasures_of_congress/text/page19_text.html
7   American System Henry Clay.

DOI: 10.1057/9781137527813.0008

6

America's Founding Economic Rights Today: Modern Government

Abstract: *This chapter interrelates the American founders' assumptions of basic economic rights with those of John Quincy Adams, Jackson, Lincoln, the populist progressives, Theodore Roosevelt, Perkins, FRD, and Martin Luther King, Jr. Also examines the New Deal's unrealized legacy in terms of economic rights in the 1960's and afterwards.*

Keywords: George Mason; Second Bill of Rights

Miller, Stephen Paul. *The New Deal as a Triumph of Social Work: Frances Perkins and the Confluence of Early Twentieth Century Social Work with Mid-Twentieth Century Politics and Government.* New York: Palgrave Macmillan, 2016. DOI: 10.1057/9781137527813.0009.

More than the first woman cabinet member and the architect of the 1935 Social Security Act, more than being the vital link between the first progressive presidency of Theodore Roosevelt and the defining liberal presidency of Franklin Roosevelt, Frances Perkins connects pressing 20th and 21st economic concerns with the American founders' most sacrosanct socioeconomic principles. By being in the vanguard of what Franklin Roosevelt calls "modern"[1] government, Perkins affirms the economic rights implicit in the June 12, 1776 Virgina Declaration of Rights enunciation of "equally free and independent...inherent rights" by George Mason that the Declaration of Independence, the Constitution, and the Bill of Rights appropriate:[2] "All power vested in, and consequently derived from, the people...magistrates are their trustees and servants and at all times amenable to them...[and] cannot, by any compact, deprive or divest their posterity; namely, the enjoyment of life and liberty, with the means of acquiring and possessing property, and pursuing and obtaining happiness and safety."[3]

"The earth belongs in usufruct to the living," says Jefferson. Jefferson's use of the Roman legal term "usufruct," meaning that it is permissible to use another's property if that property is not diminished, reflects the manner in which positive economic rights are based in the foundation of American government.[4] Similar considerations of property belonging to posterity reflect Jefferson's ideas about land and resources' ultimate collective ownership. Tellingly, Mason links posterity with property and happiness, and Mason's summation of rights as "life and liberty, with the means of acquiring and possessing property, and pursuing and obtaining happiness and safety" is halfway between John Locke's "life, liberty, and property" and Thomas Jefferson's "Locke's life, liberty, and the pursuit of happiness." Jefferson portrays more conventional private ownership as a form of stewardship for posterity and the present wider community. After all, the Constitution purports "to promote the general welfare" of America and not merely advance isolated pockets of prosperity.

The Virginia Declaration of Rights promotes positive economic rights in the sense that John Stuart Mill later distinguishes negative individual rights essentially guaranteeing the right "be left alone" from positive rights guaranteeing assistance. The Virginia Declaration of Rights announces, "The people have a right to uniform government," and "No man, or set of men, is entitled to exclusive or separate emoluments or privileges from the community," which remain animating American principles. However, Michel Foucault posits that the post-World War

II intermeshing of the national welfare state and the consumer-driven economy is the crowning achievement of societal disciplining and self-disciplining and self-disciplining for which the prison panopticon is one model. By this logic we might assume that Foucaultian thinkers would wish to be free of the governmental Social Security "structure," to use FDR's word when signing the 1935 Social Security Act that the New Deal forges. However, deleting governmental and social responsibility from economic workings would not seem to promote Foucaultian freedom or liberty. Indeed, the post-1960s prospect of such a turn from government constitutes a kind of Hegalian antithesis leading to a synthesis emphasizing the inescapability of a New Deal structure so that there is now little that is more liberal or progressive to propose than a generous and creative expansion of Social Security within the institution of well-run government work programs to counter cultures of long-entrenched poverty and artificially imposed unemployment and underemployment based upon the profits of technological advances in production not being shared with workers.

In 2008 it is only New Deal-related benefits that spur consumer demand and thwart a Depression of 1929 dimensions.[5] Similarly, eighteenth century thinkers such as Adam Smith would never propose abdicating society's duty to regulate the economy, preferably through moral and religious means but conceivably through other methods. In fact, the nineteenth century Social Darwinism with which "postmodern" neoconservatives identify opposes the ideas unleashed by Smith and other Scottish Enlightenment thinkers. Significantly, a late 20th century sense of a coming free market dominance is being replaced not with an opposing ideology of a governmentally planned economy but rather with the mixed economy that Theodore Roosevelt, Frances Perkins, and Franklin Roosevelt believe to be America's only alternative. If as Foucault implies we are now nearing the perfection of modernism it is as the dominance of the mixed economy that Foucault intimates by linking post-New Deal government with our consumer society. In many ways, Perkins and FDR are the first two practicing postmodernists, TR's New Nationalism not winning the day in 1912.

Importantly, the Virginia Declaration of Rights' last two articles voice positive rights that government must guarantee its people, thus undermining misunderstandings from both the left and the right concerning the purely negative nature of American constitutional rights and consequently linking the New Deal to America's founding assumptions.

DOI: 10.1057/9781137527813.0009

"No free government, or the blessings of liberty, can be preserved to any people but by a firm adherence to justice, moderation, temperance, frugality, and virtue and by frequent recurrence to fundamental principles," reads the Virginia Declaration of Rights' penultimate government mandate. Mason thus enunciates the qualities of civic virtue that Montesquieu requires of effective government. "Adherence to justice" is presumed to include economic justice. After all, the revolution is fought for economic equality as the founders think of it. Mason similarly invokes Montesquieu's demands upon government for "moderation, temperance, frugality, and virtue and...frequent recurrence to fundamental principles" in the sense of being effective and non-tyrannical government. FDR, more than Perkins, might well read into the words "firm adherence to justice, moderation, temperance, frugality, and virtue" a rationale for limiting personal income, which he proposes during World War II but for which he receives virtually no congressional support and then angrily denounces Congress as more "greedy than needy." After all, according to Perkins, FDR sees no need to be more than moderately wealthy, as he indeed enjoys being, though he is never worth more than a very limited number of millions of dollars.

TR's and FDR's "un-ideological ideology" is the default position of the pre-Civil War American republic, despite incorrect and widely accepted contrary claims. For instance, even before the Constitution is drafted, Congress serving under the Articles of Confederation sets aside approximately one thirty-sixth of all public lands for the states to utilize for public education. The portion of land this "land grant" mechanism provides is soon doubled. By 1862, this principle evolves into the Morrill Land Grant Act, which Lincoln promotes and signs, providing land grants making it possible for states to establish affordable institutions of higher education such as Cornell, Michigan State, and Clemson. These college land grants are analogous to Thomas Paine's late eighteenth century social insurance plan proposed for nascent industrial societies such as Britain and France and a future industrial United States. Paine's plan grants a single payment of about fifty thousand dollars in today's currency, collected from land and inheritance taxes, and given to twenty-one-year-olds. The mid-nineteenth century Land Grant Act similarly counters a scarcity of free land with subsidized higher education.[6] Similarly, the United States' 1862 Homestead Act provides free land to more than a million farmers who are able successfully to work their land for five years.

DOI: 10.1057/9781137527813.0009

In short, land is a safety valve against what Jefferson calls "pauperism" in America. Founders from Jefferson and Madison and Paine to Adams and Hamilton see no alternative to government and private enterprise cooperation in the American people's best interest.[7] Until the Civil War an abundance of land provides a modicum of prosperity for most Americans, and basic political rights are thus better articulated than economic rights. Strikingly, when the Industrial Revolution changes this and poverty becomes a given of American life, most Americans continue to deny the existence of any poverty in the United States and blame the poor themselves for their plight. This contributes to a continuing indifference to poverty in America that, in Martin Luther King, Jr.'s words, is "utterly callous to the suffering and misery of tens of millions of Americans, both black and white."[8]

That economic rights and guarantees are not better constitutionally articulated and enshrined can be partially explained as the reinforcing of a mindset underlying American slavery and the second-class citizenship of African Americans and others. Substantiating this explanation, the European poverty existing from at least the times of the serfs is not as easily denied. Thus Western Europe is initially more successful in instituting the kind of inclusive post-World War II "welfare state" that the New Deal initiates before the war. Of course this statement must be qualified because African Americans are not full partners in the New Deal since various aspects of Social Security are initially prejudiced against blacks in that farm and domestic workers are at first excluded from the old-age pension system. Nonetheless, FDR correctly considers the 1935 Social Security Act a "structure" that indeed does form the basis for more equitable inclusion, and, despite African American leadership's exasperation with Roosevelt for opting for the more pragmatic legislative route of cooperating with key Southern congressional committee chairs, FDR's popularity amongst the African American electorate, in part for simply recognizing the issue of poverty and in part for not seeming racist, as Hoover does appear, is crucial in shifting African American support from the party of Lincoln to the Democrats.

In America the genocide facilitated by ethnic nationalism that the Allies ostensibly oppose contributes to a new visceral awareness of national inclusion. However, World War II also results in a greater one-to-one European alignment of ethnicity and nation. Europe's postwar exclusion of perceived national strangers eases the institution of an inclusive welfare state in a manner that racism in the United States makes difficult. Postwar American prosperity as compared with the shambles in which the war leaves Europe also results in a greater European recognition of economic needs although FDR and the New Deal trailblaze the recognition of economic rights for Europe. More recently, as foreign workers become an undeniable presence, unworkable austerity measures threaten the European welfare state.

As in post-World War II Europe, the New Deal is probably assisted by its benefits being distributed within an ethnically majoritarian unity because post-World War I anti-immigration laws limit the number of newly arrived immigrants so that more fully assimilated Americans receive most New Deal benefits. And yet, since the 60s while Social Security becomes part of the American concensus, the right increasingly attacks parts of Social Security addressing poverty.

On February 6, 1968 Martin Luther King, Jr. sends a confidential letter to President Lyndon Baines Johnson. In "demand[ing African Americans] inalienable rights to life, liberty, and the pursuit of happiness," King's Southern Christian Leadership Conference asserts the economic right of all Americans to humane and equitable employment, income, housing, education, health care, and full political participation. It is rarely understood how specific and developed King's plan is for instituting economic rights based upon the principles of America's founders.

In effect, King's assassination two months later cuts short King's attempt to align the civil rights movement with FDR's Second, or Economic, Bill of Rights. "We demand an economic and a social Bill of Rights," says King. King's more pronounced assertion of a new bill of rights would have sharpened the 1960s counterculture's focus giving it a unifying message it lacks. "What," King asks Johnson, "is the right to live of black children who are born to be hungry and whose very minds and spirits are maimed by the savage conditions of their existence?" King rhetorically explains to the president that the social meaning of the mid-1960s race riots that mystify Johnson after his strenuous efforts to pass the 1964 and 1965 Civil Rights Acts: "What is it that the young people in the streets have a right to—a life of unemployment and low pay when there is work?" King insists that African Americans not wait another two hundred years after the 60s Civil Rights Bills to make the same kind of economic progress that the 60s begins to bring to African Americans. And yet, says King, "The rights upon which we insist do not apply only to our own people." "America," says King, "will tear itself apart" through all manner of economic inequality. Mere "dead-end jobs" will not suffice.

DOI: 10.1057/9781137527813.0009

Citing statistical evidence, King says, "There are literally millions of creative, public service jobs which could be opened up for the poor at a minimal cost and in short order...these are not make-work employments; they are new careers." Perkins believes government work programs necessary even in prosperous times, and King sees them as a necessary tool for eradicating the legacy of slavery.

Significantly, chief among King's "demands [is] acceptance on principle of the economic and social Bill of Rights." King invokes the legacy of the New Deal by calling for "direct societal guidance and intervention...shared socially." His emphasis upon "guidance" recalls Frances Perkins's wish to use government to "conference" and educate. After all, government must have a place in modern society. Certainly, it is not enough simply to trust government; mechanisms allowing for some degree of confidence in government must be established. Invoking Perkins's conference method, King calls for "the statutory right" of those affected by legislation "to play a significant role in how it is designed and administered." In this regard, King advises "a massive effort to upgrade the education available to the black and white poor."

"Without guaranteed medical care under the Social Security system," writes King, extending upon the progress made by Medicare and Medicaid, "even those who are not poor can[not] really possess the inalienable rights to life, liberty, and the pursuit of happiness." Economic inequality, says King, denies an inclusive "American Dream" not only to the poor but also to everyone else.

Martin Luther King Jr not only calls for a second American bill of rights, but also for a second New Deal; his vision intermingles the two. Although King wishes to redirect funds from the Vietnam War to finance his plan, he adamantly argues that the United States can afford to implement his plan even while waging the war King opposes. He asks Johnson and the federal government to "immediate[ly] begin...work on a racially and socially integrated model city for 250,000 citizens"; expand its program of building decent housing for the poor; and, reflecting Perkins's dedication to accurate and useful statistics, give "instructions to the Secretary of Labor making the Sub-Employment Index, which gives a much truer picture of the plight of the poor, a monthly regular statistic published by the government."

Crucially, King prescribes a minimum income chained to the cost of living but not as a complete replacement for aid to the disabled. Providing convincing statistical evidence, King demonstrates the inequity inherent

DOI: 10.1057/9781137527813.0009

in the government's subsidizing of white "suburbs" in preference to the black "ghettos." King asks Johnson to launch "a Marshall Plan," costing the same 3% of the Gross National Product that Truman pledges to Europe. King would have Johnson make "a similar commitment for the reconstruction of the United States." Tellingly, George Marshall unwittingly prepares to help revitalize Europe by administering the domestic Civilian Conservation Corps (CCC). Again invoking FDR, King states, "There must be a peacetime 'GI BILL' for the young men and women of this country, matching "the most imaginative, and profitable, social investments in the history of the United States." There must be a "passage of an Emergency Employment Act...to cover the creation of 250,000 career jobs in health, public safety, recreation...housing and neighborhood,...beautification and other fields of human development and public improvement during 1969."

Although King characterizes this as an "emergency employment act," it is revealing that King envisions it as creating "careers" rather than "jobs." For Lyndon B. Johnson, King outlines a governmental philosophy in which work programs are, as Frances Perkins's 1935 "Report of the Committee on Economic Security" to FDR says, a vital and "necessary supplement." "In periods of depression public employment should be regarded as a principal line of defense. Even in prosperous times it may be necessary, on a smaller scale, when 'pockets' develop in which there is much unemployment." Perkins's report, setting the stage for the 1935 Social Security Act, requests "employment assurance" and "differentiated treatment" also assisting those "on the verge of relief." Direct job creation, says Perkins, should not only be an "emergency measure" but "public policy" and an aspect of "broad planning" for "public construction of all kinds," and not only jobs "necessary for running the government," particularly including "programs that can directly help children." Interestingly, Perkins also maintains that these jobs should be constructive and those unable to do them should be dismissed.[9]

The founders also entertain problems of social inequality, as does Thomas Paine, living in Europe and facing the problems of post-revolution France where abundant American land does not function as the great national equalizer. Paine thus conceives a comprehensive social security system for France.

Due to the abundant resources that America's western lands provide, Marx exempts the United States from the fate of undergoing inevitably violent class warfare that he predicts for Europe's advanced industrial

DOI: 10.1057/9781137527813.0009

nations. The United States, theorizes Marx, might be exceptionally capable of peaceful and gradual social progress. After all, the American proletariat is new, industrially created, and not tied to a long feudalist past. For Marx, the United States's self-defining democratic myth might indeed extend to economic justice in the industrial age. Indeed, the New Deal constructs a uniquely American virtually non-ideological framework for mixing socialism with capitalism that with pre-World War II Sweden provide models for post-World War II Europe.

Theodore Roosevelt does not need to cherry pick American history to support his belief that the American people's best interests far supersede the narrow ideological concerns of either an imaginary "pure" capitalism or a corresponding socialism of absolute government ownership. For Perkins, pure capitalism obviously does not address many kinds of massive and unnecessary suffering and a completely planned socialist economy would be inordinately impractical and inefficient for a large nation such as the United States. Franklin Roosevelt becomes increasingly conscious of both capitalism's and socialism's interdependence, and the New Deal knocks down the imaginary wall put up by "doctrinaire capitalists and doctrinaire socialists" supporting their respective mythological "realms of either-or," as Arthur M. Schlesinger, Jr. terms it.[10]

The New Deal is a revelation of an "ideology degree zero" that is built into the American republic. Although an aversion to "ideological either-or" becomes anything but a default American political mindset, the New Deal institutionalizes "ideological aversion" to unworkably pure capitalism and socialism as the most fundamental constituent of the American political unconscious, forming an inviolable limit, or a kind of "third rail of American politics," as Tip O'Neil says about Social Security in the 1980s.[11]

In the 1960s, the New Deal's bipartisan consensus within American government breaks down when the Vietnam War with some justification undermines the faith in government that Franklin Roosevelt, together with Frances Perkins, Harold Ickes, and many others establish. FDR realizes that the New Deal requires government credibility and his presidency succeeds in avoiding major corruption and scandal. There are relatively minor charges of corruption but remarkably little is substantiated. In the 60s, however, the left and right both distrust government and afterwards American political will weakens.

The Vietnam War and Martin Luther King's assassination help to block a realization of FDR's Economic Bill of Rights and Four Freedoms.

DOI: 10.1057/9781137527813.0009

If the United States does not get caught in the maw of Vietnam, opposition to which redirects Martin Luther King's influence, and if King lives long enough to articulate his program for instituting a second economic bill of rights, a clearly defined second New Deal might ensue. Similarly, when FDR dies in 1945, Vannevar Bush, the World War II Manhattan Project's administrative director, says that this is the worst time for FDR to die because the reason for fighting the war still needs to be articulated (For Bush, this means advancing peaceful means of scientific development such as constructing systems that utilize, in Vannevar Bush's term, "personal computers" that are "networked" for research and cultural purposes in what we come in the 1990s to know as the World Wide Web. Bush believes that Roosevelt would back this project and the Web might happen decades before it does.). If Vannevar Bush might not necessarily portray the war as a struggle for economic justice and rights, Franklin Roosevelt clearly does, as demonstrated by the GI Bill's educational rights and FDR's second bill of economic rights.

One might consider the progressive legislation from the mid-60s to mid-70s, including the work of the Office of Economic Opportunity, Head Start, Legal Services for the Poor, Job Corps, Vista, Medicare, Medicaid, the Higher Education Act of 1965 including Title IV, the EPA, and the Clean Air and the Clean Water Acts, as a second New Deal. Indeed, all these programs succeed. However, they do not lead to what King calls an "acceptance on principle of the economic and social Bill of Rights." If the deaths of Roosevelt and King delay this acceptance, it may nonetheless be inevitable.

In the late sixties, Senator Robert F. Kennedy says the United States cannot address its deepest problems until it disengages from the Vietnam War. Though still addressing these deep problems, King would in large part agree. However, as I discuss in *The Seventies Now: Culture as Surveillance*, a significant American consensus never manages politically to disengage itself from the Vietnam War because it does not assimilate the war's lessons concerning the limits of force and uncritical power.[12]

In Fredric Jameson's terminology high-water modernism must exhibit self-consciousness to become effectively "late modern."[13] However, a critically late modern political aspect of the sixties remains largely unassimilated. Although the stylistic and cultural influence of the sixties saturates the nation, post-sixties politics accepts more far-right truths. In a still unresolved and ongoing post-1960s, this continuing bifurcation between culturally relaxed sixties culture and pre-New Deal and indeed

DOI: 10.1057/9781137527813.0009

pre-progressive era truisms of political and economic power wherein neoconservative opposition to guaranteed economic rights and social dignity is incorrectly assumed to be the default American position.

In the last half of his presidency it becomes clear to FDR that the nation's surplus of land and resources has long been morphing into the American economy's might, and, as Jefferson and Paine deeply believe, these resources in great part belong to all Americans. FDR therefore assumes that all Americans can and should flourish within the newly thriving and relatively egalitarian economy that the New Deal's principles forge.

The assumption of inviolable economic rights, based on the recognition of a vibrant American middle class's dominant default position, informs American history. This perspective, virtually unchallenged by America's founders, relies on early America's abundance of free or affordable land fostering prevalent wellbeing and relative "equality." America's prosperity distinguishes it from other British possessions such as Ireland, and the American rebellion surprises Great Britain.

American prosperity renders the feudal notions upon which English aristocracy is based absurd to Americans, and a visceral and often un-philosophical sense of equality fuels the American Revolution and instills respect for a strong middle class in the American character. In fact, most Americans are slow to acknowledge the very possibility of the socially generated poverty that the Industrial Revolution, growing urbanization, and business's effects on farming create. Theodore Roosevelt is the first president to confront these modern and industrial American problems through what he considers modern and industrial means. Roosevelt's Square Deal and New Nationalism reassert a default American assumption of economic rights that is only interrupted after the Civil War. Whereas TR affirms government as a positive agent of economic rights, the founders, relying on an easy access to land, concentrate on curbing a potential tyranny's usurping of economic rights. And yet presidents such as Jefferson, John Quincy Adams, and Lincoln also acknowledge government's crucial role in aiding the economy. Although Andrew Jackson opposes government's interaction with the economy, he does so based on his interpretation of Jeffersonian ideas intended to safeguard a manner of economic equality and non-favoritism. However, as president Jefferson does not act upon this interpretation, and the Whig Party forms in large part against Jackson's mode of economic inaction mitigating government investment in the American infrastructure and economy. It is from

DOI: 10.1057/9781137527813.0009

these anti-Jackson economic principles that Lincoln begins to form his economic and political precepts.

For the first time after a shift in power from the president to the congress following Abraham Lincoln's assassination, TR expressly utilizes the presidency as the prime agency of the American "people." "This is essentially a people's contest,"[14] says Lincoln about the Civil War, and, he famously justifies the war as the federal government's establishment of individual over states' rights constituting "a new birth of freedom" reaffirming "government of the people, by the people, for the people."[15] Theodore Roosevelt, whose father meets Lincoln and in TR cultivates a reverence for Lincoln extols "Lincoln democracy; the democracy of the plain people, who are honest and possess common sense," and Roosevelt says his love of Lincoln causes him "to try to be good-natured and forbearing and to free myself from vindictiveness."[16]

Lincoln of course says he fights the Civil War to preserve the union, and he explains the importance of saving the union by equating the permanence of the American union with the individual rights assumed by the Declaration of Independence and culminating in a "nation conceived in liberty and dedicated to the proposition that all men are created equal", the proactive efforts of "we the people" forming the Constitution (and before that implicitly the Articles of Confederation), and the subsequent nineteenth century broadening of the voting rights franchise. "Ballots," reasons Lincoln, are more powerful than mere "bullets." "Ballots are the rightful, and peaceful, successors of bullets," Lincoln says, and "when ballots have fairly, and constitutionally, decided, there can be no successful appeal, back to bullets."[17]

A nation powerful enough to hold democratic elections, deduces Lincoln, is also powerful enough to put down an insurrection. Indeed, the Confederacy holds almost no such elections. "The people," argues Lincoln, are the Union's only sovereigns, and the Union is the people's only avenue to power. Of course, Lincoln is rightly best remembered for his role in terminating slavery. However, for Lincoln ending slavery is a byproduct of preserving a union that in turn preserves the primacy of the people's interests. Near the close of the Civil War, Lincoln is less guarded about acknowledging slavery as the key cause of the Civil War and the abolishing of slavery advancing the national good. In his second inaugural address, Lincoln reasons that the overwhelming sacrifices of the war serve to repay in some manner what we might call a collectively "karmic"

DOI: 10.1057/9781137527813.0009

debt. Still, freeing slaves serves the people's wellbeing and supposes a direct and intimate relation between the president and the people.

Theodore Roosevelt similarly believes himself to be battling for the people. This is why he launches the New Nationalism with a speech in Osawatomie, Kansas, where John Brown helps instigate the Civil War. However, for TR, the struggle is primarily for the poor and working class. If President William McKinley promotes expansionist foreign policy to protect foreign markets for the supposed interests of everyday Americans, Roosevelt not only extends this reasoning by expanding the president's role in both foreign and domestic affairs. In this sense, Roosevelt philosophically succeeds Lincoln as much as McKinley. Like Lincoln, Theodore Roosevelt explicitly uses federal power in the public interest. Lincoln and Roosevelt both contend that the people's interest justifies giving the president the constitutional benefit of the doubt. Though TR sees no explicit constitutional power for setting the radical precedent of mediating the 1902 Pennsylvania Coal Strike, he believes this action crucial for the nation's wellbeing.

TR believes the people charge the president with unique powers as their sole steward. Roosevelt of course coins and epitomizes the term "bully pulpit" as the president's direct channel to the American people. However, a strong president such as Andrew Jackson seeks to save the people from the government and also (like TR) the special interests that it can serve. On the other hand, Lincoln engages in positive governmental functions in addition to putting down insurrection, and Roosevelt seeks government power to regulate large corporations, conserve land and resources, and provide social and economic security. Not coincidentally Roosevelt follows Lincoln in assuming executive order-based powers that Lincoln adapts to preserve the union and TR employs to preserve resources. Ironically, Roosevelt attempts to curb the ill effects of the industrial order that the Civil War facilitates, and TR, like FDR afterwards, believes it necessary to appropriate some measure of socialistic reform to forestall more radical government upheaval and the possibility of another national, now class-based, insurrection.

Substantiating the symbolic significance of six-year-old Theodore Roosevelt's witnessing of Lincoln's New York funeral procession down Broadway, Roosevelt is the first president to pick up Lincoln's thread of presidential activism and relatively direct consideration of the American people. The Civil War aside, Lincoln envisions the federal government's instrumental role in an expanding American economy. When Lincoln

DOI: 10.1057/9781137527813.0009

comes to the House of Representatives in 1845, he is elected on a Whig program of federal aid for education and the improvement of the national transportation infrastructure in a manner that is consistent with all presidents before Andrew Jackson. As president, Lincoln resumes the pre-Jackson presidential function of advancing internal improvement. And yet after Lincoln no American president until Theodore Roosevelt assumes this to be his duty.

Lincoln helps pass both the Homestead Act, allowing acquisition of land in the West in exchange for the labor of settlers developing that land, and the Morrill Act, donating land to states to establish mechanical and agricultural colleges. He also supports the construction of the transcontinental railway. In addition, although TR does little to advance racial justice, Roosevelt does make great strides in other forms of social and economic justice, and it should be noted that Lincoln also helps pass laws enabling African Americans to serve as witnesses in federal courts, outlawing Washington, DC streetcar discrimination, and permitting Jews to serve as chaplains in the army. Lincoln also revokes Grant's order to expel Jews from the general's Tennessee operations.

The Fourteenth Amendment reflects Lincoln's legacy as pivotal in the nation's shift from a tacit to an active and explicit guarantee of constitutional "equal protection" under the law since the concept of equal protection necessitates a positive governmental role and a swing from negative Bill of Rights terminology such as "shall make no law." In the twentieth century, the Fourteenth Amendment's equal protection clause comes to apply the Bill of Rights to individual state law, and the clause continues to determine Supreme Court decisions such as in the June 26, 2015 Supreme Court ruling that universalizes gay marriage rights. However, by positing the rights of certain "phantom personhoods," the Fourteenth Amendment has also served a wide array of less progressive purposes such as establishing the personhood of corporations in the nineteenth century, and in more recent years stopping the counting of the Florida vote in the 2000 election and in providing for the protection of "personal freedoms" allowing corporations to discriminate against women's health needs and in overwhelming the financing of political campaigns by striking down campaign reform. In a similar manner, before the New Deal the Sherman Anti-Trust Act is used to suppress union activities and strikes for "restraining trade." However, despite a twisting of the intentions of the Fourteenth Amendment and the Sherman Anti-Trust Act, the amendment's acknowledgement of the need actively to protect

DOI: 10.1057/9781137527813.0009

individual and collective rights and the Sherman Act's recognition of government's positive role in fighting economic inequities fOrecast a reconfiguration of American government.

If TR is the first post-Civil War president explicitly acting in the American people's direct interests, President Grover Cleveland exemplifies the pre-TR stance by saying that a president cannot act directly to end the Panic of 1893 since "government functions do not include the support of the people."[18] Contrastingly, Roosevelt takes an active hand in encouraging J.P. Morgan to quell the Panic of 1907. Of course, Cleveland's statement that government does not support the American people is absurd on its face. How can government not serve people? After all, the Constitution's preamble claims power from "the people...to form a more perfect union." However, Cleveland voices reverence for deferring to a particular understanding of Adam Smith's "invisible hand" reinforced by laissez faire Social Darwinism according to which the economically strong should not be checked for the general good, and thus "government functions" serve the workings of wealth and neither the middle or working class nor the poor, since *directly* serving the weak would also weaken the nation.

This indirectness is much different from that of the founders but may seem in accord with them because of the founders' reluctance to act in the direct interests of particular constituencies, which are associated with hated feudal notions of an aristocratic system of favors and anathema to revolutionary ideals. Nonetheless the reticence of early American politicians to be reflexively proactive creates the illusion of a default laissez faire American position. The manufactured consensus of a post-Civil War ruling Social Darwinist ideology is challenged by populism, progressivism, socialism, and the Theodore Roosevelt and Woodrow Wilson presidencies, but the renewal of laissez faire ideology after World War I makes its re-questioning seem once again new during the Great Depression.

After Cleveland, President William McKinley displays a presidency that is newly active within foreign affairs. Following McKinley's 1901 assassination, Roosevelt pledges to continue the late president's policies. However, the anthracite coal strike of 1902 in Pennsylvania demonstrates Roosevelt's extension of federally activist policies into the domestic realm. In demanding both sides to settle, Roosevelt associates "the crying needs of the people" with "the general good."[19] Previous presidents do not take the interests of workers into account when considering the general

DOI: 10.1057/9781137527813.0009

good as it relates to labor strikes. Indeed Andrew Jackson, Rutherford B. Hayes, and Grover Cleveland deploy soldiers to break up strikes.

In sharp distinction, the term Square Deal acquires literal meaning when Roosevelt engineers a deal or settlement between the coal operators and workers—the federal government's first overt efforts to mediate a labor strike. Roosevelt's role in appointing the commission to settle the coal strike empowers workers if not explicitly unions and greatly advances labor's general bargaining position. The settlement leads to establishing a nine-hour day. Further, labor activity and strikes are legitimated and boost union activity. Samuel Gompers calls the strike's settlement "the most important single incident in the labor movement in the United States...from then on the miners became not merely human machines to produce coal but men and citizens.... The strike was evidence of the effectiveness of trade unions."[20]

On October 3, 1902, Roosevelt claims to "speak for neither the operators nor the miners but for the general public."[21] The Square Deal thus establishes the presidency's role as an arbiter advocating not so much for the average worker as for that worker's implicit right to "a fair hearing," thus positing the federal government as an implicit guarantor of due process regarding economic rights. It does not matter to Roosevelt that he cannot find an express constitutional power for presidential mediation of a labor conflict. He decides that it is more important that it is not expressly forbidden. Much as Lincoln gives precedence to a national emergency, Roosevelt says he would rather be impeached than see the nation without coal in the winter.

The Square Deal also furthers the concept of the general wellbeing, and in this sense "economic rights" is paramount to government actions through Roosevelt's role in controlling corporations and protecting average farmers and business people. At the end of the nineteenth century there is massive consolidation of corporate capital and power into "trusts." Roosevelt believes government must combat "the manifest evils of the trusts" as "malefactors of great wealth" and he establishes a consensus for the government's place in this fight.[22] TR's administration prosecutes restraint of trade suits against companies such as the Northern Securities Company in the railroad industry and the "Beef Trust" in the meatpacking industry. Indeed, TR's actions cause the Supreme Court to declare the breakup of holding companies constitutional and the court also reverses itself on its previously complete exclusion of the manufacturing sector from the Sherman Anti-Trust Act.

DOI: 10.1057/9781137527813.0009

TR orders that immense areas of land be saved from railroad, industrial, and other private investment interests. He is instrumental in establishing the nation's Forest Service and a magisterial national park system. Roosevelt irrigates dry western lands through the 1902 Newlands National Reclamation Act of 1902. Importantly, he also establishes the Federal Bureau of Corporation that eventually leads to the Federal Trade Commission. TR helps pass measures speeding anti-trust prosecutions and the 1903 Elkins Act forbids special railroad rates for companies offering kickbacks. Roosevelt's Square Deal morphs into something like TR's post-presidential New Nationalism during his second term with the 1906 Hepburn Act's railroad supervision, 1906 establishment of the Food and Drug Administration and Roosevelt's increasingly activist efforts to conserve resources and enshrine national parks, preserves, and monuments.

More directly than the Square Deal, the New Nationalism equates the general wellbeing with the protection of a dynamic middle class's economic rights. Roosevelt's view of a Square Deal increasingly shifts from emphasizing a balance of interests between labor and capital to government's attempts to advance the average American worker's welfare. Roosevelt's 1912 New Nationalism is a dramatically new kind of "progressivism."

Strikingly, popular approval of the Roosevelt presidency's activism achieves a national consensus. Roosevelt dramatically breaks from the relatively stagnant domestic agenda of every president since Lincoln. In 1904, he was reelected in an unprecedented landslide, TR trounces Democratic candidate Alton B. Parker who runs to Roosevelt's right and represents a party faction that at times seems most concerned with wresting power from populist William Jennings Bryan, the previous two presidential election's Democratic standard bearer. Startlingly, however, in 1908 the Republican candidate, William Howard Taft, is able to make the agenda of Bryan, again the Democratic candidate, seem irrelevant by running on Roosevelt's record. After Roosevelt steals Bryan's thunder by enacting populist initiatives such as railway regulation, the nation settles into a "progressive/populist" amalgam tilting progressively. In remarkably innovative fashion, Roosevelt's presidency for the first time demonstrates the president's ability to deal energetically with labor rights, conservation, the avoid of a major recession, and fight interstate commerce abuses. In 1912, Taft attempts to run to Bull Moose candidate TR's left. Taft professes his greater concern for working people by attacking TR for as president dropping an anti-trust suit to break up US

DOI: 10.1057/9781137527813.0009

Steel, although Roosevelt had already begun to favor regulation over the dismantling of trusts. ("You can't unscramble an egg," he notes.) Thus, in 1912, virtually all the votes go to Wilson, Roosevelt, and Taft, running as progressives, and to Socialist candidate Eugene V. Debs who receives the other 6% of the vote. However, this progressive consensus falls apart after World War I. A new consensus forms around a "return to normalcy," but in 1929, the floor falls from beneath this normalcy.

Notes

1   Perkins, *Roosevelt*, p. 13.
2   US National Archives Records Database, http://www.archives.gov/exhibits/ charters/print_friendly.html?page=virginia_declaration_of_rights_content. html&title=NARA%20%7C%20The%20Declaration%20of%20 Independence%3A%20A%20Transcription
3   Ibid.
4   Thomas Jefferson, *Letters to James Madison* (September 6, 1789, Paris): http:// www.let.rug.nl/usa/presidents/thomas-jefferson/letters-of-thomas-jefferson/ jefl81.php
5   James K. Galbraith, *The End of Normal: The Great Crisis and the Future of Growth* (New York: Simon and Schuster), p. 187.
6   http://www.ssa.gov/history/paine4.html
7   http://founders.archives.gov/documents/Jefferson/03-07-02-0471
8   All quotes from Martin Luther King, Jr. below are from http://www. thekingcenter.org/archive/document/economic-and-social-bill-rights
9   Frances Perkins, Chair, "Report of the Committee on Economic Security," 1935, pp. 7–8.
10 Schlesinger, vol III, p. 647.
11 Marc L. Goldwein, *Riding the Third Rail: The Politics of Social Security Reform in the Retrenchment Era*, April 24, 2007. pp. 1. http://dx.doi.org/10.2139/ ssrn.1007811.
12 Stephen Paul Miller, *The Seventies Now: Culture as Surveillance* (Durham, NC: Duke University Press, 1999).
13 Fredric Jameson, *A Singular Modernity: Essay on the Ontology of the Present* (New York: Verso, 2002), p. 197.
14 Kenneth Stampp, *The Causes of the Civil War: Revised Edition* (New York: Simon and Schuster, 1990), p. 69.
15 Abraham Lincoln, "The Gettysburg Address," November 19, 1963. http:// www.abrahamlincolnonline.org/lincoln/speeches/gettysburg.htm
16 Kathleen Dalton, *Theodore Roosevelt: A Strenuous Life* (New York: Alfred A. Knopf, 2007), p. 207.

DOI: 10.1057/9781137527813.0009

17   Abraham Lincoln, Speech c. May 18, 1858. *The Collected Works of Abraham Lincoln*, ed. Roy P. Basler, vol. 4, p. 439.

18   Grover Cleveland, "Second Inaugural Address," March 4, 1893. http://avalon. law.yale.edu/19th_century/cleve2.asp

19   Jonathan Grossman, "The Coal Strike of 1902—Turning Point in US Policy." *Monthly Labor Review* (October 1975).

20   http://www.dol.gov/dol/aboutdol/history/coalstrike.htmSamuel Gompers, *Seventy Years of Life and Labor, An Autobiography, Volume II* (New York, E. P. Dutton & Co., 1925), pp. 117, 126–127.

21   Theodore Roosevelt, "Letter, Roosevelt to H. H. Woodward, October. 19, 1902," in Elting E. Morrison (ed.), *The Letters of Theodore Roosevelt, Volume III*, pp. 356–357(Cambridge, MA: Harvard University Press, 1951).

22   Kathleen Dalton, *Theodore Roosevelt: A Strenuous Life* (New York: Alfred A. Knopf, 2007), p. 253.

DOI: 10.1057/9781137527813.0009

7
The New Deal as the Social Work of Desire

Abstract: *This chapter discusses the New Deal's reconfiguration of artistic modernism and early American applications of economic rights so as to incorporate a new vision of social work.*

Keywords: cubism; Federal Children's Bureau; Florence Kelley; Martha Nussbaum; modernism; modernist art; Walter Benjamin

Miller, Stephen Paul. *The New Deal as a Triumph of Social Work: Frances Perkins and the Confluence of Early Twentieth Century Social Work with Mid-Twentieth Century Politics and Government*. New York: Palgrave Macmillan, 2016.
DOI: 10.1057/9781137527813.0010.

On the evening of February 22, 1933, New York State Industrial Commissioner Frances Perkins hesitates as President-elect Franklin Delano Roosevelt confirms rumors he intends to nominate her as his Secretary of Labor. Perkins believes she can accomplish more in New York than she ever could in Washington, even though the position she occupies is only the state equivalent to the federal one the President-elect offers at his East 65th Street home. Perkins feels uncertain as Roosevelt interviews prospective Secretary of the Interior Harold L. Ickes, whom Perkins only identifies as someone who is definitely not urbane enough to be a New Yorker. However, Perkins herself feels "very green and ignorant about all aspects of the government except the thing I knew about."[1]

What Perkins "knows" are meticulous details about New York workers and workplaces. After her landmark stewarding of the state committee investigating work hazards after the 1911 Triangle Shirtwaist Factory fire and then her leadership of the New York Industrial Commission, an agency growing out of the fire's investigation, she can apply her research to curbing hazards at work and improving working conditions. However, there are few if any precedents in the federal government pertaining to the workplace regulations she has already instituted in New York. The United States Supreme Court considers such work unconstitutional in rulings that generally prevent state minimum wage laws from infringing upon Fourteenth Amendment contractual rights. At the same time the court uses an overly restrictive reading of the Tenth Amendment, originally intended to prevent the federal government from assuming absolute powers, but then used to stop the federal government from regulating child labor. When drafting the Tenth Amendment, James Madison attempts to avoid such misinterpretation by striking "expressly" from "expressly delegated"ca so that it reads: "The powers not delegated to the United States by the Constitution, nor prohibited by it to the States, are reserved to the States respectively, or to the people." Certainly, the federal government's power to regulate interstate commerce allows Congress to impose a tax upon furniture made by children when sold out of state. However, the Supreme Court decides this federal power is unconstitutional because not expressly given to the national government even though Madison expressly does not use the word expressly. The Supreme Court thus limits the powers of the federal government by imposing on it the kind of restraints that John Stuart Mill terms "negative" rights, but it does so by denying the child laborers and other

DOI: 10.1057/9781137527813.0010

workers the "positive" right not to be overworked, seriously ill-treated, or endangered by their working conditions.

Significantly, it is not only the conservatives on the court who over-rule federal legislation regulating the workplace. Progressives fear "big government" as much as "big business," and progressive justices such as Louis Brandeis and Oliver Wendell Holmes, Jr. vote with the majority in the 1922 *Bailey v. Drexel Furniture Company* of North Carolina decision curbing the federal government's ability to restrict child labor since the production of the furniture in question involves in-state sales. However, while the Supreme Court invalidates federal child labor laws for improperly interfering in intrastate commerce, the court regularly strikes down state child labor, minimum wage, maximum hour, and other labor laws for perceived contract-to-labor violations based on the court's reading of the Fourteenth Amendment. Similarly, the 1918 *Hammer v. Dagenhart* Supreme Court decision rules that the federal government's power to regulate commerce does not extend to the production of goods and therefore child labor cannot be federally regulated.

In the face of this judicial impasse, Richard Hofstadter's *The Age of Reform* documents how after World War I prohibition and anti-immigration efforts absorb much of the progressives' energy.[2] In addition, exhaustive research by Otis L. Graham, Jr. concerning the political perspectives of early twentieth century progressives who survive into the New Deal reveals that "old progressives in surprising numbers" do not join in "the return of reform hopes under Franklin Roosevelt."[3] Most pre-World War I progressives, excepting those involved with early social work, are not preoccupied with abject poverty. Social workers are the progressives who most vehemently oppose poverty, and they also will be the progressives with the fewest ideological inhibitions about government directly confronting poverty during the New Deal. According to Graham, it is primarily the social workers "who preferred the risks of character damage through federal relief to the very real miseries brought about by the Depression." As previously noted New Deal emergency relief work programs and the 1935 Social Security Act, says Graham, "satisfy the most deeply rooted desire" of an early twentieth century social worker such as Perkins.[4]

Frances Perkins's career bridges a generally indirect American view of the federal government's economic responsibility with a more targeted and definite economic function. How can we understand the roadblocks Perkins faces against implementing such a direct approach on the federal

DOI: 10.1057/9781137527813.0010

level? Relating an indirect governmental tack as it impacts poor children will be useful in this regard.

One of President-elect Franklin Roosevelt and Perkins's first exchanges at Roosevelt's home on February 22, 1932 demonstrates the chasm between indirect, or general, and direct particular applications of government. Perkins responds to Roosevelt's Secretary of Labor job offer by noting that little "had ever been done about working people, or working people's problems, or labor legislation in the Department of Labor."[5] She recalls "pointing out that...the Children's Bureau's activities, although happily lodged in the Department of Labor, had nothing particularly to do with working people." Her use of the word "particularly" is telling because the bureau is initially conceived *particularly* for the children of the poor and working class.

The federal Children's Bureau is a 1903 brainchild of social workers Florence Kelley and Lillian Wald who reason that if agriculture warrants a government agency then the interests of children, especially poor ones, also certainly do. Kelley and Wald convince President Theodore Roosevelt to support the establishment of a federal children's agency. Although the two social workers are specifically concerned with the interests of poor children, the 1912 law that the Congress passes and President Taft signs creates the federal Children's Bureau to investigate and report "upon all matters pertaining to the welfare of children and child life *among all classes* of our people" (italics added).[6]

Perkins thus tells FDR, "Most children who need the ministrations of the Children's Bureau are the children of poor people.... It should become a poor people's department."[7] Indeed, demonstrating the potential controversy embedded within Perkins's view, the 1935 Social Security Act, for which Perkins is the legislative architect and chair of the Committee on Economic Security drafting the Act, charges the Children's Bureau with housing the Act's Aid to Dependent Children provision, a provision many Americans still equate with their negative view of "welfare."

Even in the 1930s many surviving progressives such as Carl Vrooman, Graham Taylor, William Allen White, and Oswald Garrison Villard oppose most federal safety net measures. "When the New Deal recognized and dealt with particular social groups," observes Graham, "it undid the work of years of progressive effort, for it divided rather than united the American people."[8] Most progressives resist anything that looks like special treatment for either the rich or the poor.

DOI: 10.1057/9781137527813.0010

After all, it is difficult for government to own up to and justify acting directly on behalf of particular individuals or groups. For instance, in Congress such assistance is often associated with "earmarks," or "specified targets" for government largess, typically placed deep within laws to avoid notice and scrutiny. Earmarks seem quite nefarious even when bringing effective action because even the appearance of justified favoritism goes against the visceral sense of equality and fair play that in large part motivates the American Revolution. Government thus most often does well to appear neutral and indirect. As Alexander Hamilton's 1789 federal plan to establish the full faith and credit of the United States meets resistance because it gives a boost to the nation's creditor class, proposals by early twentieth century social workers directly to assist the poor through government are suspect and rarely implemented. Most Americans at that time view poverty as a personal and not a societal problem, and as Martha Nussbaum says, "People who have the idea that the poor brought their poverty upon themselves by laziness fail, for that reason, to have compassion for them." However, even when poverty is acknowledged compassion for the poor may not be deemed an appropriate governmental motive. "Is compassion a threat to good political thinking and the foundations of a truly just world community?" asks Nussbaum. After all she observes, compassion has an "obvious propensity for self-serving narrowness."[9] Not one, however, to forsake compassion, Nussbaum sees an indeterminate solution to the kind of problem that many pre-New Deal Americans discern in a "dialectic" of "critical compassion."[10] If many early twentieth century Americans do not even exercise critical compassion for the poor, most of the founders nonetheless promote relative economic equality by maintaining a broad national distribution of land ownership, and the not always articulated yet mighty drive toward "equality" generating the American Revolution includes a crucial economic dimension.

Before returning to Perkins and FDR at his townhouse on East 65th Street, a short digression concerning equality, land, and governmental indirection will shed light upon the ambivalence that Perkins feels concerning joining the federal government when she feels the need for direct government action. An early American imperative necessitating a loosely defined implementation of "equality" based on land supposes a kind of "economic equality." Of course, no two Americans are absolutely equal. Slavery is also a glaring exception. However, if slavery can possibly be put aside, early Americans would be galled by a government's aggressive perpetuation of inequality. If the founders empathize with a large spectrum of Americans, the Constitution's framers nonetheless suspect government workings that are not "neutral and indirect." Like Nussbaum, they prefer government that critically distances its compassion. The Constitution thus prohibits the proportioning of a Congressional district with fewer than thirty thousand inhabitants. In 1787 America, this is an exceedingly large number of people. (In the early twentieth century when Congress limits itself to 435 members, it guarantees an even more remote ratio of the represented to the representative. Now a typical House member represents more than a half of a million people.)

The founders theorize that a representative's perspective should be balanced and checked by many vested interests. Similarly, the ancient Greek democratic system draws representational precincts so as to include diverse countervailing interests forcing constituents to entertain diverse viewpoints. Among the institutions devised to separate the government from its people are the Electoral College, the electing of United States senators by state legislatures (until the Seventeenth Amendment) that are in themselves "malapportioned" until the Supreme Court's 1960s "one man, one vote" rulings, and winner-take-all elections for Congress contrasting with the multi-representative apportionment of a single district's representation following an election in other countries. Single-winner Congressional elections create a one-to-one relation between "land-units" and their representatives. American winner-take-all elections work against more pointed and direct third party interests. In short, the founders see neutral and remote government as an aid to good, proper, and rationally self-critical governmental process. Compassion must be critical.

There is a bias toward considerations of land in this government's remoteness. Tellingly, the closest that the United States has ever come to calling a second Constitutional Convention in the manner that the Constitution prescribes comes in the aftermath of the Supreme Court's "one man, one vote" decisions. Although the justness of these decisions now appears self-evident, the fierce opposition these rulings originally meet testifies to the import of land within the national psyche.

In the 1960s, a Southern state such as Georgia is determined to stick to its "unit rules." A unit rule keeps districts in place regardless of changes in population. Thus, for example, Atlanta's growth does not affect its representation. Land, not population, matters. It is as if each district were

DOI: 10.1057/9781137527813.0010

a state represented in the United States Senate, its number of legislative representatives eternally fixed. As unjust and horrifyingly unrepresentative as this system is, it does prevent gerrymandering. Unit rules therefore do evince simplicity and dignity. Perhaps a weighing of land over people harks back to a time when America is predominantly rural and most American families own land. As speculative as this observation seems, it nonetheless accounts for two American mysteries. First, why is it that only America goes to war about slavery—a war in which American causalities exceed that of all other American wars combined? Why do Southerners fight for a way of life they associate with slavery when the great preponderance of Southerners do not own slaves? Could it have something to do with Southern slavery being psychologically equated with a prosperous rural economic life? Whereas in other nations land ownership is a source of strife, it has more equitable and positive associations in America. Second, why even now does a presidential election map show a Republican candidate victorious in much greater swaths of landmass even when a Democrat wins? Could it be that members of the party more psychologically invested in preserving a vision of the past tend to find themselves in or gravitate to more sparsely inhabited lands because an abundance of land is associated with the past?

When FDR meets Frances Perkins on February 22, 1933 on New York's Upper East Side, New York City has become the world's preeminent city due to an influx of gold and financial trading, and Perkins has been a New Yorker for twenty-seven years. When she sees future Secretary of the Interior Harold Ickes for the first time being interviewed by Roosevelt, she looks down on him for not looking like a New Yorker. As a New Yorker, she also looks down on the federal government's indirect stance. In weighing FDR's offer, she is more concerned with making the job of Secretary of Labor a relevant one than with affecting any ideological shift. In claiming to be not knowing about "government except the thing I knew," Perkins assumes a stance that will allow the New Deal to cut an ideological Gordian knot so as to do what must be done.[11]

Perkins proposes something very difficult. She says she will accept the job only if Roosevelt supports her in turning the Labor Department into a significant government agency. Beyond constitutional challenges, Perkins associates this 1933 "period of terrible depression" with a time when "people don't want to spend any money."[12] In 1932 Roosevelt campaigns upon his intention to balance the national budget. In addition,

DOI: 10.1057/9781137527813.0010

although some economists have begun to consider the possibilities of compensatory spending, John Maynard Keynes has yet fully to formulate its benefits. Perkins thus sees little alternative to austerity. She therefore cannot see how even one relatively modest condition for accepting the position, such as Roosevelt's support in her remaking of the Office of Labor Statistics into a relevant and reliable institution, can possibly be funded. "We'll have to completely reorganize and revise the Bureau of Labor Statistics, shake it all up and get it on a decent and effective level. Will you support it because *it will cost money*?" (italics added) asks Perkins, and Roosevelt answers, "Yes."[13]

Perkins is further perplexed because she does not "know how much [Roosevelt] cares about some of these things, which I care about a great deal.... I did not know then actually how deeply his heart was involved."[14] She reasons that although she works well with Governor Roosevelt in New York State government, most of the groundbreaking state programs that she helps to plan and administer are either accomplished under previous governors or, as for instance in the case of state unemployment insurance, are not yet legislatively formulated when Roosevelt becomes president. Perkins is also uncertain because her state position is not only less politically problematic and potentially more productive than its federal counterpart. The state job also pays more, and her move would be a serious burden for her family since her husband suffers from what is now understood as a debilitating bipolar mental illness and her daughter, whose life is later disrupted by a similar mental illness, is comfortable in her New York school. Relocating will be a major chore. She only wants to accept Roosevelt's cabinet position on her own terms. In the twenty-four hours between Roosevelt's summoning of her and their meeting, Perkins articulates to herself her prerequisite conditions for taking the job-jotting each demand on a pad. FDR must support what she wishes to do in a wide array of areas including federal government work programs (though her demands are minor in comparison to what FDR himself will demand in only about a month), strengthening the Labor Department, old-age pensions, child labor regulation, minimum wages, maximum hours, workers' compensation, unemployment insurance, and—the only condition not realized under Perkins and FDR's tenure—universal health care. "I think I ought to tell him what I want to do and I ought to put it to him—does he want those things done?" Perkins wonders. "Because if he embarks with me, this is the kind of advice he'll be getting."[15] It is thus Roosevelt and not Perkins who must pass the audition.

DOI: 10.1057/9781137527813.0010

In a very direct fashion Perkins sums up her suspicions about Roosevelt. "I did not," says Perkins, "know how deeply he gave a damn about whether the working girl's back ached or not." To exemplify her ambitions in government she therefore recounts the exaltation she experiences at "the great victory" in revising a state law mandating seats for workers. "We had been able to amend the law so that not only should women be provided with seats in their places of employment, but they should be provided with seats with backs," says Perkins. FDR "roar[s] with laughter that I should think that was a victory," recounts Perkins, causing her to "stand" and "denounce him." "You don't know anything about women's backs," she scolds the President-elect. "They ache like thunder from sitting up perfectly straight at a machine with no support for the small of the back." According to Perkins, Roosevelt "looked at me in bewilderment as I gave him a kind of an angry lecture on the subject" going into great detail about a Long Island factory doing an end-run around the law requiring seats by taking "seats off the harvester machine—one of those iron seats." This "killed the girls.... They were better off standing."[16]

Near the end of the interview, Perkins asks FDR if he will support each of her initiatives "because you won't want me for Secretary of Labor if you don't want those things done. I'd be an embarrassment to you," says Perkins, "because when I start on a thing, I round up the cohorts." She clarifies her process so he knows what to expect. "I get out advisory committees who really become supporters of the idea," she says. "You get a public demand for it the next thing you know. You wouldn't want me if you didn't want that done."[17] Although Roosevelt agrees to support Perkins's agenda, she still doubts her time in the president's cabinet will be worthwhile.

Her recognition of the importance of a woman being represented in the president's cabinet probably has more to do with her taking the position than her expectations of any great achievements. After all, notes Kirstin Downey, "No European or American woman before Francis had ever played such a high-profile role in public life, unless within a hereditary aristocracy or because of a sexual liaison."[18] And yet though she believes Roosevelt will support her, she cannot expect success in the face of entrenched institutional and cultural challenges. These roadblocks come from both the left and the right since most progressives, though supportive of curbing the powers of big business, oppose the American government's direct interaction with its people and for the most part

DOI: 10.1057/9781137527813.0010

with the economy. Although they may favor anti-trust enforcement, campaign and government reform, and food and drug regulation, progressives generally oppose other innovations and want to preserve an America they can recognize. There is little context for a national government rising to meet the economic demands of its people.

What accounts for this antipathy toward government's direct engagement with its constituents? John Kenneth Galbraith provides a clue to a possible answer. Galbraith maintains that World War I marks a "turning point of modern economic history" unleashing much political and economic confusion that over time affects whom governments represent.[19] Despite Marx's assignation of economic power to European industrial capitalists, says Galbraith, aristocrats rule European government until World War I. Galbraith notes that before the war it is "still a serious social and political disqualification to be 'in trade.' Businessmen, financiers, went their own way. It was not the natural function of those so engaged to govern."[20] Similarly, in Henry James novels such as *The American* and *The Ambassadors*, how one earns a living or amasses a fortune is simply not to be mentioned. However, the authority of European aristocrats is severely brought into question when they instigate and bungle World War I, killing and maiming large percentages of young Europeans.

Land, says Galbraith, is at the heart of a mindset informing pre-World War aristocracy, politics, and government. From a colonialist perspective, acquiring land through imperial conquest is of unquestionable value. In America too land distinguishes the nation's leaders and the process for selecting them. This raises two overarching points. First, although land relates differently to European and American governments, the tangibility of land and the processes though which land ownership is valued, developed, utilized, and protected is nonetheless crucial to both the prevailing European and American political mindsets. Second, whereas in Europe land provides a cultural marker for the division of classes, the American founders envision land ownership as an agent of democracy and political reconciliation. Psychological associations with land are vital to the development of American economic rights. For example, Thomas Jefferson never advocates universal white male suffrage but in 1776 Jefferson indirectly promotes just this by proposing that all white males in Virginia should possess at least fifty acres of land, and if a white man lacks that number of acres the difference should be given to him.[21] For Jefferson, this would tweak small problems occurring within what in

DOI: 10.1057/9781137527813.0010

1786 he called, "the lovely equality which the poor enjoy with the rich."[22] Crevecceur had after all previously cast Americans as "united by the silken bands of mild government" in "a pleasing uniformity" in which "absolute poverty worse than death had been banished."[23] While abundant land makes America's "lovely equality" possible, in 1795 Thomas Paine, diverging from later Social Darwinism, equates economic equality with a default and "natural" position of abundant land. Paine believes a lack of land makes equality far more difficult in Europe. "It is always possible to go from the natural to the civilized state, but it is never possible to go from the civilized to the natural state," says Paine. "The reason is that man in a natural state, subsisting by hunting, requires ten times the quantity of land to range over to procure himself sustenance, than would support him in a civilized state, where the earth is cultivated."[24] However, Paine devises an ingenious remedy to European and later American land scarcity and economic equality, something much like America's later Social Security.

On August 7, 1787, the Constitutional Convention also demonstrates an affinity between democracy and land (sometimes amongst other property considerations). John Dickinson has an ironically democratic-leaning rationale for supporting Governor Morris's proposal that the Constitution impose land ownership as a qualification for members of the Congress, or "national legislature," and the Electoral College. "The great mass of our Citizens," Dickinson explains according to James Madison's minutes, "is composed at this time of freeholders, and will be pleased with" the requirement that they own land.[25] Dickinson's claim that most Americans, unlike most people in Great Britain and the United States, do in fact own land is indeed true. Despite the existence of slavery in the United States, from a numerical perspective land and property ownership qualifications for both government service and voting are less anti-democratic than they are within Europe since a much greater percentage of Americans own land. The founders do not impose specific federal land or property qualifications for the same reason that they oppose such prerequisites, but rather they wish to avoid unnecessary conflict with the states by setting a divisively uniform standard of land and property ownership and tax payment when property requirements for voting and serving within state legislatures differ from states to state. George Mason observes, "Eight or nine States have extended the right of suffrage beyond the freeholders, what will the people there say, if they should be disfranchised," and, after all, it can be argued that property,

DOI: 10.1057/9781137527813.0010

capital, and taxpaying are sufficient criteria for voting. In addition, Pierce Butler cautions his fellow founders not to play with fire because "there is no right of which the people are more jealous than that of suffrage."[26]

Nonetheless, land is the kind of property that most Americans own, and it is therefore a relatively democratic sufferance requirement. That a little more than a decade later Jefferson's Republican Party, with a base of farmers and landowners, becomes much more popular than the Federalists, who come to represent commercial, financial, and manufacturing interests, attests to the widespread character of land ownership. Therefore, according to Richard Hofstadter, the founders base the nation's relatively democratic workings on "the broad dispersion of landed property."[27] This is in effect the rationale behind the House of Representatives, which is first elected in 1788 by primarily landowners. Land ownership therefore contributes to the American electoral tradition, and, in the early American republic, owning land is considered to be a chief guarantor of economic rights. What better safety net can there be than owning land? Land ownership is thus the lynchpin of the Jeffersonian Republican agenda.

And yet Jefferson's party says Hofstadter, "offered no guide to a specific agrarian program. They had no plan; indeed they made a principle of planlessness," and there is something reassuringly American about this principle.[28] However, by the late nineteenth century, there is still an underlying "planlessness" within otherwise momentous populist and progressive plans. Although innovative and valuable, populist and progressive programs are largely conservative in the sense that they seek to preserve or to reestablish outdated pre-industrial capitalist conditions. The breaking up and regulating of large corporations and progressive transparency initiatives within political campaigns and governments seek to limit the influence of big business so that America can be as it once was perceived to have been—a nation of small businesses and farms on a smaller scale.

And yet there is little in the way of planning for how the federal government can positively safeguard the people's minimal welfare and enrich the quality of Americans' lives, or, for that matter, utilize the benefits of business, manufacturing, and agriculture on a large scale. Although populists and progressives wish to break up cartels and the concentrated wealth of huge corporations, and the 1912 Bull Moose Progressive Party platform boldly advocates universal health insurance and other positive goals for the federal government, socialists put forward some

DOI: 10.1057/9781137527813.0010

manner of planned economy, and populists propose nationalizing the railroads, nonetheless populists and progressives in many ways stand for the restoration of a pre-industrial capitalist ownership based on a relatively equitable distribution of land and property that no longer exists. Americans before the New Deal are given relatively few choices between laissez faire and a planned economy. And yet before the New Deal there is unarticulated ambivalence. In 1922 William Carlos Williams writes, "So much depends upon a red wheelbarrow," implying a reliance upon a sort of democratic every person bespeaking traditional progressivism and populism. However, the poem also suggests that this little man or woman deserves and may need the help of a larger community of "glazed rainwater" and "white chickens."[29]

After the New Deal it is difficult for radicals of either the right or the left to imagine anything but a mixed economy. By 1940 Perkins observes, "It seemed to me that our program was now bipartisan. Nobody would ever abandon Social Security. Nobody should ever abandon the regulation of hours and wages, the prohibition of child labor, and all that kind of thing. That was done. I had accomplished what I had come to do."[30]

It is hard now to recognize how "radically moderate" the mixed economy of the New Deal initially is. After all, an economic "mix" is less catchy than either a magical invisible hand of capitalism or the historical inevitability of Marxist class struggle. And yet in terms of such inevitability, Karl Kautsky's analysis of about a hundred years ago, "Our task is not to organize for the revolution, but to organize ourselves *for* the revolution; it is not to *make* the revolution but *to take advantage of it*," cannot seem as done a deal to us as to Kautsky.[31] Similarly, we may wonder if the "patience" Lenin professes always guides him.

Michael Harrington observes that in the 1930s the only liberal democratic influences moving beyond an "either/or" relationship between capitalism and socialism are Keynes, the New Deal, Swedish socialism, and some forns of French socialism.[32] Intriguingly, Harrington reconsiders nineteenth century socialism so as to entertain an alternative view of socialism and Marxism interacting with capitalism, a mixed economy regulating capitalism through the democratic means that capitalism, says Marx, fosters after feudalism.[33] In fact, before World War I Henry Ford, thinking as a capitalist, anticipates the New Deal and Keynes by putting a relatively high floor beneath the wages he pays his workers to guarantee the existence of consumers to buy his product. There is no clear line between concentrated wealth and its relatively egalitarian distribution.

DOI: 10.1057/9781137527813.0010

In fact, a "relatively egalitarian" mixed economy would seem requisite for any healthy modern economy. Simply put, if modern societies would be impossible to manage without some socialist organization (the military after all is a form of government organization despite more recent and problematic privatizations of the American military such as Blackwater), it is nonetheless difficult to plan an entire national economy, or for that matter to imagine an entire government withering away. From a more right wing perspective, President Reagan's first budget director, David Stockman, may call Social Security "closet socialism," but he and Reagan abandon plans to drastically alter Social Security.[34]

A consideration of what is surprisingly "radically mixed" about the New Deal should not mitigate what is vital and meaningful about progressivism but rather underscore unconscious and conscious progressive barriers that work with obvious conservative opposition against what Perkins and the New Deal ultimately accomplish. Progressives nevertheless achieve the Sherman Anti-Trust Act, the Pure Food and Drug Act, direct elections of United States senators, women's suffrage, and a progressive income tax. And yet progressives are electorally repudiated after World War I. Even in New York, Al Smith loses his governorship in 1920 only to sweep back into office in 1922 when New York becomes an outlier for a new kind of progressive paradigm prefiguring the New Deal although not entirely anticipating every vital New Deal element such as compensatory spending, the huge scale of its work programs, and many features of Social Security.

Considering the crowded agenda and significant achievements of pre-World War I progressivism it is clear how other important items, such as direct remedies for poverty and advancing the civil rights of minority groups, do not reach the top of their agendas. It is as difficult as it is absurd to "go back in time and judge" turn of the twentieth century progressivism since much that it overlooks is still overlooked. The populists and progressives are after all to be credited for recognizing in industrial capitalism an opponent in large part responsible for the exponential growth of poverty even if most progressives do not then fully come to terms with poverty's existence.

In the nineteenth century, land ownership dovetails with perceived American values. Landed proprietors naturally feel a responsibility for their surroundings while business people focus more on the bottom-line. Most relevant to this study, understanding the achievements and the shortcomings of the progressive movement helps to clarify why Frances

DOI: 10.1057/9781137527813.0010

Perkins's direct involvement with workers and citizens is difficult to conceive on a federal level against the backdrop of a government working within a tradition basing democratic reform upon the protection of land and property rights.

"The central faith of American political ideologies," says Hofstadter, is "the sanctity of private property" developing into "a beneficent social order" with "a strong bias in favor of equalitarian democracy."[35] Faith in the property's sanctity is easier to understand in terms of land. Even in the depths of the Depression, says Perkins, "On the farm, with a roof over your head and some skill, you can still get something to eat usually."[36]

Perkins observes that before becoming president FDR has difficulty distinguishing an impersonal industrial corporation from "an English gentlemen" upon his farm, one who wishes to know "if the crops went wrong or the sleet storm came at the wrong time." As "the gentleman who ran the estate had other sources of income [and] a lot of blankets, a lot of food and a lot of other things, and he took it for granted that it was his duty to distribute those."[37] According to Perkins, Roosevelt needs to discover the manner in which most corporations first and foremost value profit.

The New Deal must break through a seemingly sensible notion of government impartiality to accomplish targeted reform counterintuitively in the interests of practically all Americans. Part of the difficulty is that though in later decades both Milton Friedman and Richard Nixon acknowledge "We are all Keynesians now," Keynes does not begin to work out what Keynesianism means until after World War I when he theorizes that the compulsion of the Allies to economically punish Germany and Austria-Hungary for World War I inadvertently also devastates their own Allied economies. Similarly, most do not feel it is in their interest to help the poor. If politics and economics can be seen as ways for people and nations to get along together for the benefit of all, as Keynes ingeniously demonstrates, most still do not fully grasp this concept now. In many ways, despite the obvious inconsistency of accommodating slavery, the founders do seem to grasp this idea.

However, though land ownership can be viewed as a progressive and democratic feature of the United States' Jeffersonian "democratic party," this perspective sheds light on why an American government conducted in this tradition is slower to recognize the need for setting up safety nets than are the governments of Europe. Since in America

DOI: 10.1057/9781137527813.0010

land ownership is more of collective virtue that it is in Europe, Americans have a harder time seeing through property rights to the need for direct government involvement within the lives of people. In Europe however the voices of unions and advocates of the poor and working classes are more understandable. After all, traditions of aristocracy are not based upon equal and neutral government treatment. Therefore, in 1880s Germany, Bismarck helps pass legislation establishing workers' health insurance, disability compensation, and old-age support. By the early twentieth century, other European nations, including Britain, have similar programs.

Despite these reforms European governments still primarily represent the interests of landed aristocracy, and, according to Galbraith, World War I demolishes any basis for the credibility of a previously dominant political tradition based upon land ownership. The values of a landed aristocracy reflecting the feudal system are still ensconced in European government. Jean Renoir's film *Grand Illusion* demonstrates this by a French World War I prisoner of war equating his status as a Frenchman with owning an "acre" of land, and Renoir's *The Rules of the Game*, made right before World War II, depicts an aristocracy shown to be essentially useless though still dictating the rules by which society lives. Renoir presents a lifeless aristocracy able to accomplish little except its own control. Indeed, war itself may be a mode of such control. "Only war," says Walter Benjamin, "makes it possible to mobilize all of today's technical resources while maintaining the property system."[38] Near the end of *Grand Illusion*, a character identifies the "grand illusion" as the hope that World War I will be the last war. Renoir introduces a later edit of *Grand Illusion* by saying that the only answer lies in human relations. For Renoir, human affections trump not only narrow national but also class interests. Although a German officer in charge of a prisoner of war camp nobly feels a POW's status as a gentleman to be more important than the nation he has fought for, he nonetheless assumes all German officers are opposed to Jews. However, the film's Jewish POW is valorized though he characterizes himself as a "naturalized Frenchman" from many lands. In other words, he is not from the right *land*. And yet this is made to be something of a positive, or at least a mode of survival, as he and the French POW with whom he has bonded escape into an indefinite "no-man's land" of snow. Consciously or unconsciously, Renoir suggests that through an uncritically applied manner of the zeitgeist's operation the war can be considered in part as the European aristocratic governing

DOI: 10.1057/9781137527813.0010

elite's last gasp stand to assert and retain power. Of course, this unusual explanation is merely one of a number of possible conscious and unconscious reasons for the war, such as Germany's and the Austro-Hungarian Empire's search for oil and other fuels.

World War I roughly coincides with the late 1913 use of the assembly line to produce Model-Ts. This age of mass production detracts from the aura of an aristocratic class. Aristocratic characters in *Grand Illusion* and *The Rules of the Game* bemoan their "vanishing privileges" as the latter film puts it. These aristocratic fears foreshadow how Andy Warhol later describes the 1960s, as a kind of classless party in which everyone drinks the same Coca-Cola and watches the same television shows and movies. In *The Rules of the Game*, the radio and the airplane thus psychologically challenge the aristocracy's sense of their superiority. After all, this aristocratic superiority is felt to be "on the ground" with actual land as Picasso writes *"Notre Avenir est dans l'Air"*—"Our Future is in the Air"—on his 1912 painting, *The Scallop Shell*, challenging aristocratic values.

If European aristocracy loses its luster, America's democratic impulse loses its base in reality. Nineteenth century "industrial capitalism," says Hofstadter, "sunder[s] democracy from the farm.... It has sundered four fifths of society from the soil, has separated the masses from their property, and has built life increasingly on what Jefferson would have called an artificial basis," deleting the "practical content" from an original formulation of American democracy.[39] The disintegration of a seemingly "real" basis for the economy and the prevailing political system is problematic for European aristocrats and American progressives alike. In the 1930s, Walter Benjamin identifies a similar "decay of aura," by which he means the eclipsing of the authentic atmosphere of the unique work of art due to the ascendency of photographed images, filmed movement, and recorded sound.[40] "To pry an object from its shell, to destroy its aura," says Benjamin, "is the mark of a perception whose 'sense of the universal equality of things' has increased to such a degree that it extracts it even from a unique object by means of reproduction."[41] Benjamin evokes Picasso's intense yet subtle painterly and visual analysis in *The Scallop Shell*, prying the object of a scallop shell into a reduplicating environment of multiple scallop shells.

Benjamin posits both loss and opportunity in the aura's collapse. Although Benjamin expresses an unbridled pleasure with which the aura of the unique art object can be enjoyed, he maintains that transcending the un-reproducible art object engenders a "sense of the universal

DOI: 10.1057/9781137527813.0010

equality of things" and makes the cultural participation of most workers possible, and Benjamin notes that the births of photography and socialism are historical doublets of the late 1830s.[42] In the early twentieth century, film and the industrial mass production of the assembly line, which we have already noted as a historical doublet of World War I, further trump aura's authority. It is important to note that Frances Perkins becomes a celebrity in this historical moment through the attention she gives to codifying statistical details concerning workplace conditions. Significantly, Benjamin foresees Perkins's manner of statistical analysis while working within New York government as a new mode of reproductive "art." In the federal government, Perkins professionalizes the Office of Labor Statistics. Reduplicating an "object" so as "to destroy its aura," says Benjamin, "manifest[s] in the field of perception what in the theoretical sphere is noticeable in the increasing importance of statistics. The adjustment of reality to the masses and of the masses to reality is a process of unlimited scope, as much for thinking as for perception."[43] Benjamin thus contextualizes Perkins's conceptual art.

In comparison to Europe, the United States's less bloody and more efficient war effort, posits Galbraith, reinforces a Civil War sense of the North's industrial capitalism (over Southern land ownership), later backing the World War I Allies. The war transforms America into central world economic player. New York becomes crucial not only for the rest of the country but also for the entire world.[44]

New Yorkers are led to see a new kind of reality. Tammany Hall breaks through democratic modes psychologically limited by the sway of land ownership to a government engaging with its people. Tammany leadership realizes that they must appeal to the poor and working classes to maintain their political control, and they enlist Frances Perkins to this end. How does this democratic impulse concern Perkins's focus on minute details involving the everyday worker? What does recognizing the inadequacy of progressive and aristocratic mindsets have to do with the delight Perkins takes in, for instance, legislating not only seats for workers *but also backs* on those seats? Certainly Perkins exhibits laudatory empathy with what workers must endure. However, the directness and the materiality of focus upon concrete details that Perkins wishes to bring to the federal government reminds us that her career blossoms in a period of artistic modernism that begins reaching its high point in the years immediately before World War I. During these years Galbraith argues that world politics and culture anticipates the wartime revelation

DOI: 10.1057/9781137527813.0010

of aristocratic rule's emptiness, and after the war this emptiness is contextualized and codified.

Is there a relationship between modernism and government's distinction between chairs with and without backs? If so it must concern a heightened sense of detail characteristic of modernism. One thinks of the for its time unusual opening of *The Rules of the Game*. Instead of introducing a location or character through any kind of traditional establishing shot, we see radio cables. This is an establishing shot introducing process and technological context. Similarly, as Cubism concerns the paradoxical bonding of an isolated detail to a totalizing yet open flat field, so Perkins engages in a comparably "totalizing yet open" statistic field relentlessly blending the real and tangible features of working conditions.

It may seem cavalier to group so many artistic, cultural, and historical phenomena together as modern or modernist. The rationale for so doing is threefold. First, so many of the early twentieth century modernists are contrary—Eliot, Williams, Pound, Stevens, and Stein for instance exhibit deep oppositions—that it seems unwise to look for a definitive criteria for excluding forcefully and conceptually processed work from the category of the modern. Second, "forcefully and conceptually processed work" merits consideration for being "modern" if only because such work exhibits something bespeaking what appears to be an epistemic spirit of the age. And if epistemic and historic trends tie together what we detect as modern then, third, it is fitting to include politicians and other thinkers in the conversation about what it is to be modern. After all, Keynes, one of the most economically and politically influential people of the twentieth century, is a member of London's Bloomsbury set that reassess assumptions about human nature, and Keynes reads his writings to the predominantly literary group. In addition, in 1941 Keynes heads Great Britain's new Britain's Council for the Encouragement of Music and Arts, and he considers the "circulation" of popular art able to make the common person feel "as nothing else can, that he is one with, and part of, a community, finer, more gifted, more splendid, more care-free, than he can be by himself.[45]

Referring to Perkins as a "modernist" may also be disputed because modernism is linked with fascistic mindsets. After all, part of the "force" we identify with modernism can be linked to Nietzsche's valorizing of the exercise of power over the enervations he relates with moral choice. And yet power can also be associated with the development of physical

DOI: 10.1057/9781137527813.0010

electricity driving the age and generating a dynamic critical rationality accounting for various streams and sources of power. As Perkins and the New Deal cut the Gordian knot dividing the government from its constituents, perhaps we can also cut the knot dividing the aesthetically modern from liberal and progressive politics.

Modernism of course has roots before the twentieth century. In *Modernisms: A Literary Guide*, Peter Nicholls identifies many "modern-isms," the "beginnings" of which "are largely indeterminate, a matter of traces rather than of clearly defined historical moments."[46] Nicholls chooses to begin his account of literary modernism in the 1840s, near the advent of photography, the telegraph, and the railroad when images, communication, and transportation are mechanized and reconfigured. Correspondingly, many of Nicholls's characterizations of modernism include or concern a "grounding of the aesthetic in an objectification of the other."[47] Such objectification can however, as in Emile Deroy's "To a Red-Haired Beggar Girl" (written at about 1845), "identify" with a poem's poor lower class subject and "testify to a 'humanitarian' impulse beneath the deliberate playfulness of the poem's pastiche."[48]

Perkins similarly identifies with the humanity of the worker whom she also in a sense objectifies so as to appreciate politically and in a sense aesthetically in the "Cubist" manner, leveling "aristocratic perspective" into a flat "reverse perspective." In other words, the "window" that had looked within the painting or government code now looks out from it toward the viewers and constituents themselves.

Modernism is also often theorized by thinkers such as Gerald Graf as a nineteenth century response to the Industrial Revolution. Indeed, the moment of modernism preceding World War I when Perkins conducts her game-changing Triangle Fire investigation is one with the age of electric power stations and grids that thoroughly domesticate electricity and thus forge home and city environments that we still largely experience together with the mass assembly line-based consumption electricity facilitates. It becomes increasingly difficult to separate the consumer dimension of life in the industrial age from the comforts of the home.

In 1941, William Phillips accepts a Depression assumption concerning modern art as being innately apolitical because it is in "permanent mutiny against the regime of utility and conformity."[49] And yet such an "art for arts's sake" position precedes World War I and applies to pre-war "rules of the game." In pre-World War I Britain, for instance, the painter and poet Mina Loy must be careful not to compromise herself and her

DOI: 10.1057/9781137527813.0010

education by appearing to learn any commercial art instead of fine art.[50] Similarly, Perkins, who like Loy is born in 1882 and dies in 1965, one year before Loy's death, considers a career in painting and other fine and performing arts. However, Perkins chooses social work. Nonetheless, a career as a "settlement worker," as social workers are then often called, is a kind of "art," a semi-professional career choice considered suitable for a young woman.

After all, if social work is practical in that it assists the needy, it is also impractical in that the low wages that social work jobs pay can add to the number of poor people. It follows that early social workers live among the poor since social workers might themselves be poor. However in 1909 when Perkins moves to New York she lives in the "stimulating atmosphere" of Greenwich Village. This excitement reflects a community living within an increasingly "plugged-in" city.

Frances Perkins shares a cultural life not only with the poor but with modern artists and writers as well. Perkins, Kirsten Downey observes, "Frequented avant-garde art shows, concerts, lectures, and political rallies." Indeed, although she ostensibly comes to New York to study social work at Columbia University, Perkins is "still unaware what shape her career would take." She tries her hand at acting and writing and publishes several short stories. Perkins helps Sinclair Lewis edit *Our Mr. Wrenn*, and she refuses Lewis's marriage proposals. The New York community Perkins frequents is fluid. She befriends and interacts freely with many diverse artists, writers, politicians, and thinkers such as activist John Reed and municipal planner Robert Moses. Perkins does not limit her range of personal associations. After all, her friends, says Perkins, would never "get upset because people have" different or "funny ideas."[51] Indeed, Perkins doesnot differentiate the delight and satisfaction she receives from innovative art and politics. Perkins may thus be said to find an artistic calling in social work and then later within government.

Interestingly, in 1940 Perkins's support of Varian Fry's Emergency Rescue Committee is vital in bringing (and re-bringing) from Europe to America such artistic and cultural figures as Andre Breton, Marcel Duchamp, Andre Masson, Marc Chagall, Max Ernst, Jacques Lipchitz, Franz Werfel, Hannah Arendt, Wanda Landowska, Jacqueline Lamba, Otto Meyerhoff, Konrad Heiden, Emil Gumbel, Hans Natonek, Leonhard Frank, Alfred Polgar, Hartha Pauli, Jaques Hadamard, Lion Feuchtwanger, Heinrich Mann, Golo Mann, Hans Sahl, Wilfred Lam, Walter Mehring, and Alma Mahler. This influx of artists and related

DOI: 10.1057/9781137527813.0010

figures of course contributes to making New York the artistic capital of the world after World War II.

Unsurprisingly, it is Perkins who sets the historical precedent of suggesting that Roosevelt include various kinds of both artists and writers in New Deal emergency work programs. FDR immediately assents. Indeed, a program such as the Creative Writer's Project pays writers to work privately upon their own writing and produces work such as Richard Wright's *Native Son*.

Bespeaking the pragmatic paradigm informing the New Deal, Perkins and Roosevelt do not differentiate art and writing from more seemingly useful professions. She describes FDR "in full revolt against the 'economic man.' He didn't like that concept at all," says Perkins. "I've heard him poke fun at that. He'd say that he'd just talked to some economist and by talking to them you'd think that a man was nothing but an eating machine."[52] To an extraordinary extent, Roosevelt seems to have trouble objectivizing. Perkins says that to explain anything theoretical to FDR she must anchor ideas to concrete images. She further maintains that Roosevelt tends to personify abstract ideas such as corporations and also concrete objects, which, says Perkins, he sees "as a person. He would tend to personalize. I believe that in philosophy that is called animism." She notes, "I often caught him in what I regarded as the grave error, and even heresy, of animism, which is to personalize impersonal objects. But that was the way he could think about them."[53]

Tellingly, Perkins sees FDR as a "creative modern artist" whose modernism differs from Perkins's own peculiar modernism.[54] Perkins and Roosevelt practice respective "modernisms," as Nicholls might put it. Perkins likens Roosevelt to an "automatic writer" who proceeds by "trial and error" and not according to any "blueprint."[55] Roosevelt "usually made up his mind while talking," says Perkins. "In the use of his faculties Roosevelt had almost the quality of a creative artist." Perkins says he has "the quality of the modern artist as distinct from the classical artist . . . [He] begins his picture without a clear idea of what he intends to paint or how it shall be laid out upon the canvas, but begins anyhow, and then, as he paints, his plan evolves out of the materials he is painting." As Dewey theorizes, FDR learns while doing. His intentions are not isolated from his work process.

When Frances Perkins exhorts fellow Democrats to campaign in 1936 on their Depression emergency measures and tout them as representative of the party's lasting activism in the direct service of the American

DOI: 10.1057/9781137527813.0010

people, she renews a politics as ridiculous as the Armory Show, recalling her experience investigating the Triangle Fire. Progressivism had previously been a conflicting mix of isolated reforms tending to oppose strong or large government as much as it contests large private corporations.

Indeed, after the 1912 election and World War I, a popular association between anxieties concerning the war and the unsettling nature of social progress and appeals for more of it lead to the rejection of even traditional notions of progressivism.

Perkins helps others in FDR's administration recognize how the New Deal transforms American government, and how this accomplishment can be used politically in the 1936 reelection campaign, a campaign that FDR initially considers difficult. After all, perhaps no president had ever been elected in the face of nearly complete and unified business, press, and media opposition. "They had begun to consider the Government of the United States as a mere appendage to their own affairs,"[56] says FDR describing this opposition, echoing the Virginia Bill of Rights prohibition "That no man, or set of men, is entitled to exclusive or separate emoluments or privileges from the community."[57] Roosevelt is not being disingenuous when he says, "We know now that Government by organized money is just as dangerous as Government by organized mob." He describes his experience by observing, "Never before in all our history have these forces been so united against one candidate as they stand today. They are unanimous in their hate for me—and I welcome their hatred." He describes the New Deal's success and hopes for new levels of its success when he says, "I should like to have it said of my first Administration that in it the forces of selfishness and of lust for power met their match. I should like to have it said of my second Administration that in it these forces met their master."[58] And yet many on Roosevelt's campaign advise him to take back these remarks or risk a backlash costing him the election. However, Roosevelt, angry about Republican tactics such as employers placing notes in paycheck envelopes blaming FDR for the loss of the workers' pay to Social Security payments and instructing them to vote Roosevelt out of office, disregards this advice. As late as the weekend before the election, *Liberty* magazine's widely trusted poll shows Alf Landon defeating Roosevelt. Nonetheless, in October 1936, FDR at a wildly enthusiastic and unexpectedly large Chicago campaign rally sees signs deriding the *Chicago Tribune*, causing his inner political calculations to tell him that he has pierced through newspaper opposition and will be reelected in a landslide.[59]

DOI: 10.1057/9781137527813.0010

Why are not the New Deal's accomplishments more obvious to Democratic National Committee members before they ask Perkins to suggest rationales from which to base the 1936 election? The answer to this question is particularly difficult to ascertain in the light of new waves of misinformation obscuring and skewing mechanisms for even liberal and pro-FDR economists to determine the scope of the New Deal's success. In the late twentieth and twenty-first centuries economists have been discrediting sensible methodology for accounting for the New Deal's performance. Since the economy returns to where it is before the Depression by the end of Roosevelt's first term, the New Deal would seem to be a rousing success understandably resulting in the president's unprecedented landslide victory despite overwhelming institutional opposition. "By 1936, the United States economy had returned to its previous peak level of real economic activity, and to many, this might plausibly be counted as the moment of 'full recovery,'" says James K. Galbraith.[60] However, many economists, especially revisionist neoconservative economic thinkers such as Lee Ohanian, Harold Cole, and Amity Shales, reject this commonsense appraisal. They argue that the traditional expectation of economic growth should apply to the Depression years as if the Depression did not happen. By this standard, the New Deal is faulted for the destruction of the economy for the three and a half years *preceding* the New Deal.

As absurd as this reassigning of blame from the Hoover to the Roosevelt administration is, James Galbraith demonstrates that even an economist championing New Deal economic policies, Paul Krugman, shortchanges the New Deal by crediting World War II for ending the Depression. There are two other factors camoflaging the New Deal's triumph. First, even Frances Perkins's Labor Department statistics calculate workers within the WPA and other government work programs as unemployed. New Dealers themselves believe Americans working in government programs are unemployed and thus the Depression far from over in 1936. This also causes even "pro-New Deal" scholars such as William Leuchtenburg and Doris Kearns Goodwin to believe the millions of New Deal work program workers to be unemployed.[61] By this logic, Public Works Administration (PWA) and WPA projects such as the Bay and Golden State Bridges in San Francisco; Doubleday Field in Cooperstown, New York; Laguardia Airport; Camp David; the landmark Mathematics Tables Project which the US Navy finds invaluable in World War II and is institutionalized after the war as the

DOI: 10.1057/9781137527813.0010

National Bureau of Standards; Dealey Plaza in Dallas; and state writers' projects meticulously documenting states' geography and other features; magnificent art and literary projects by Jackson Pollock, Richard Wright, George Stanley, John August Walker, Alton Tobey, Donal Horde, Wilem de Kooning, Thomas Hart Benton, and seemingly countless others; and Chicago's fabulous Outer Bridge Drive are miraculously constructed by the idly unemployed and/or by generous volunteer help.

Second, in 1937, the Depression seemingly nearly over, Roosevelt feels he can discontinue the experiment of massive work programs and, relying upon more conventional economics, balance the budget. The result is the 1937 recession. By the time FDR reinstates the work programs in 1938 the arms build-up begins, giving the impression that defense spending, which to the Roosevelt administration's credit is doggedly carried out to benefit the cause of economic equality despite unavoidable corporate growth, ends the depression. Military expenditures are after all a manner of Keynsian compensatory spending that are made to support the New Deal's basic innovative principles through responsible accounting measures and the institution of taxes large enough, when adjusted for economic growth, to negate any ill effects of deficit spending.

Perhaps, despite the New Deal's re-simulation, in the National Recovery Administration (NRA) and during the war, of early American government and business cooperation for the public's benefit, the New Deal's success is obscured by an American inability to adapt pre-Industrial Revolution assumptions to America's industrial realities. Accordingly, most American "progressives" in the 1930s paradoxically have a retrospective and nostalgic vision for the nation's future that, says Otis T. Graham, would "restore the small-town synthesis their fathers presumably enjoyed."[62] Despite their achievements early twentieth century progressives tend to share surprisingly much with contemporaneous laissez faire capitalists. Only a relatively marginalized left remains to carry the banner for government's role within a planned economy, and for most socialists and communists the ideological basis for this belief forecloses the kind of realistic solutions the New Deal's mixed contributions of labor unions, but merely to reaffirm Perkins's strong belief that labor unions require the assistance of government legislation and administration. However, labor unions generally have few expectations for government assistance. After all, government is more likely to break up strikes then help mediate them, although TR's help in this way is a notable exception.

DOI: 10.1057/9781137527813.0010

In a sense Debs influences Theodore Roosevelt to search for viable labor-management solutions. Still, Debs's support of the government ownership of all industries is remote from TR's wish to regulate all industry, and unions such as the Wobblies are more uncompromisingly anti-capitalist than Debs. Nonetheless, mainstream progressives do not truck governmentally "socialist" solutions for poverty and other problems. Before the New Deal, except for progressives such as Perkins, who brings an early social work bent toward action over ideological inhibitions to New York State government, most progressives fear governmental "bigness," to use Louis D. Brandeis's term, as much as they fear big business, and, as many of Brandeis's Supreme Court votes siding with more conservative justices demonstrate, government's power to be thoroughly modern, pervasive, and proactive is hampered.[63]

Only when the Depression unexpectedly continues to worsen before he takes office does FDR acknowledge his fundamental duty to recognize Americans' positive economic rights. He determines that the government must do something immediate and positive to help its people. Following the example of Cleveland remark, "government functions do not include the support of the people,"[64] in 1931 President Herbert Hoover similarly maintains that "the sole function of government" is to facilitate "private enterprise."[65] Compare these two presidential pronouncements of their duty not to ameliorate the poor's present suffering with James Madison's sole contribution to the Virginia Declaration of Rights: the document's strongly worded last governmental injunction speaks for most of the founders: "That religion, or the duty which we owe to our Creator, and the manner of discharging it, can be directed only by reason and conviction, not by force or violence; and therefore all men are equally entitled to the free exercise of religion, according to the dictates of conscience; and that it is the mutual duty of all to practice Christian forbearance, love, and charity toward each other." From a twenty-first century perspective the word "Christian" is of course overly exclusive, and yet Perkins and FDR would both recognize in Madison's words their forms of secular Christian practice embodying collective responsibility while not imposing any hint of sectarian division. Although the Episcopal Church elevates Perkins to a level wherein she is celebrated each year with a May 13 feast day, in which many Episcopalians recognize Perkins for her "saintly deeds," and despite Perkins's claim to need regularly to keep silence at a Maryland religious retreat, her Labor Department assistant Thomas H. Eliot recalls few in the administration having any

DOI: 10.1057/9781137527813.0010

idea of Perkins's relation to religion.[66] Similarly, FDR says he has no other philosophical or political principles than being a Democrat and a Christian, linking the communal concern implicit in his notion of both.[67] However, Perkins and FDR recast politics "in an emotional way," as Perkins puts it.[68] Although she herself is cerebral and self-disciplined, Perkins realizes what Madeville, Hume, and Mill all theorize: desire, or underlying belief, must be harnessed as if a modernist force.

Notes

1   Columbia University Libraries, Part 7, p. 574.
2   Richard Hofstadter, *The Age of Reform* (New York: Alfred A. Knopf, 1955).
3   Graham, p. 157.
4   Ibid., p. 103.
5   Columbia University Libraries, Part 3, p. 583.
6   Social Security Administration, "The Children's Bureau," http://www.ssa.gov/history/childb1.html
7   Columbia University Libraries, Part 3, pp. 583–584.
8   Graham, p. 174.
9   Martha C. Nussbaum, "Compassion and Terror," *Daedalus*, 132:1 (2003): 10–26.
10   Ibid.
11   Columbia University Libraries, Part 7, p. 574.
12   Ibid., p. 571.
13   Ibid., p. 606.
14   Columbia University Libraries, Part 7, pp. 571, Part 7, pp. 607, http://www.columbia.edu/cu/lweb/digital/collections/nny/perkinsf/transcripts/perkinsf_7_1_571.html.
15   Ibid.
16   Columbia University Libraries, Part 7, pp. 572–573, http://www.columbia.edu/cu/lweb/digital/collections/nny/perkinsf/transcripts/perkinsf_7_1_572-3.html.
17   Columbia University Libraries, Part 7, pp. 607, http://www.columbia.edu/cu/lweb/digital/collections/nny/perkinsf/transcripts/perkinsf_7_1_607.html.
18   Downey, p. 312.
19   John K. Galbraith, *A Journey through Economic Time: A Firsthand View* (Boston: Houghton Mifflin, 1994), p. 19.
20   Ibid., p. 11.
21   Richard Hofstadter, *The American Political Tradition and the Men* (New York: Vintage, 1989), p. 41.

DOI: 10.1057/9781137527813.0010

22   Thomas Jefferson to John Banister, Jr., October 15, 1785. Boydet al., *Jefferson Papers*, XV, 396.

23   J. Hector and St. John de Crevecoeur, *Letters from an American Farmer* (1782) (New York: Dutton, 1957), Letters III and XII.

24   Thomas Paine, "Agrarian Justice," http://en.wikisource.org/wiki/Agrarian_Justice

25   The Avalon Project, Yale Law School, http://avalon.law.yale.edu/18th_century/debates_807.asp

26   Ibid.

27   Hofstadter, p. 18.

28   Ibid., p. 48.

29   William Carlos Williams, *The Red Wheelbarrow,* https://www.poets.org/poetsorg/poem/red-wheelbarrow

30   Columbia University Libraries, Part 7, p. 824.

31   Michael Harrington, *Socialism: Past and Future, The Classic Text on the Role of Socialism in Modern Society* (New York: Arcade, 1989), p. 49.

32   Ibid., p. 58.

33   Harrington.

34   Nancy Altman and Eric Kingston, *Social Security Works! Why Social Security Isn't Going Broke and How Expanding It Will Help Us All* (New York: The New Press, 2015), p. 146.

35   Hofstadter, p. xxxvii.

36   Columbia University Libraries, Part 7, p. 616.

37   Ibid.

38   Walter Benjamin, "Work of Art in the Age of Mechanical Reproducibility," in Edmond Jephcott, et. al. (trans.), Howard Eiland and Michael W. Jennings (eds), *Selected Writings: Volume 4, 1938–1940* (Cambridge, MA: Harvard University Press, 2003), pp. 251–283.

39   Hofstadter, pp. 41–42.

40   Walter Benjamin, "On Some Motifs in Baudelaire," in *Selected Writings: Volume 4, 1938–1940*, pp. 313–355.

41   Walter Benjamin, "Work of Art in the Age of Mechanical Reproducibility," in *Selected Writings: Volume 4, 1938–1940*, pp. 251–283.

42   Ibid.

43   Ibid.

44   John K. Galbraith, pp. 19–29.

45   John Maynard Keynes, "Art and the State," Part 1, *The Listener* (August 26, 1936): 372.

46   Peter Nicholls, *Modernisms: A Literary Guide*, second edition (London and New York: Palgrave MacMillan, 2009), p. 1.

47   Ibid., p. 4.

48   Ibid.

DOI: 10.1057/9781137527813.0010

49 William Phillips, "The Intellectuals' Tradition," *The Partisan Review* (November–December 1941): 482–483.

50 Carolyn Burke, *Becoming Modern: The Life of Mina Loy* (Berkeley, CA: University of California Press, 1996), pp. 35–64.

51 Downey, pp. 25–32.

52 Columbia University Libraries, Part 7, p. 609.

53 Ibid., p. 612.

54 http://millercenter.org/president/speeches/speech-3307

55 Perkins, *Roosevelt*, p. 163.

56 Franklin Roosevelt, *Address on the Second New Deal*. http://docs.fdrlibrary. marist.edu/od2ndst.html

57 http://www.archives.gov/exhibits/charters/print_friendly. html?page=virginia_declaration_of_rights_content.html&title=NARA%20 %7C%20The%20Declaration%20of%20Independence%3A%20A%20 Transcription

58 http://millercenter.org/president/speeches/speech-3307

59 Schlesinger, vol. III, p. 647.

60 James K. Galbraith, p. 190.

61 Ibid., pp. 189–194.

62 Graham, p. 181.

63 Schlesinger, vol. III, p. 647.

64 Cleveland, Second Inaugural Address, March 4, 1893.

65 Ronald Brownstein, *The Scond Civil War: How Extreme Partisanship Paralyzed Washington and Polarized America* (Penguin, 2008), pp. 48.

66 http://mountholyokenews.org/2013/04/06/frances-perkins-awarded-golden-halo/

67 Thomas H. Eliot, *Recollections on the New Deal: When the People Mattered* (Boston: Northeastern University Press, 1992), p. 101.

68 Columbia University Libraries, Part 2, p. 49.

DOI: 10.1057/9781137527813.0010

8
The First Charge upon the Government

Abstract: *The chapter places social work within the American political tradition and progressive movement. A return to the distinction between Hamilton and Jefferson informs government and big business' relationship throughout American history, giving a framework for the establishment of social work. This chapter also analyzes the government's role in business over the course of American history, outlining how presidents ranging from Jefferson to John Quincy Adams used powers granted in the Constitution to serve "business" ends in serving the economy, such as the Louisiana Purchase and Hamilton's setting up of a national bank. Historical context is given in order to illustrate the mindset of the Early American government and its relationship with business and how it establishes the groundwork for FDR's New Deal.*

Keywords: Agricultural Adjustment Administration; Democratic National Convention; government and business; Jacksonian; National Bank; Tennessee Valley Authority

Miller, Stephen Paul. *The New Deal as a Triumph of Social Work: Frances Perkins and the Confluence of Early Twentieth Century Social Work with Mid-Twentieth Century Politics and Government*. New York: Palgrave Macmillan, 2016.
DOI: 10.1057/9781137527813.0011.

DOI: 10.1057/9781137527813.0011

Social workers "operat[e] in the area where social work and politics intersect," says Arthur M. Schlesinger, Jr.[1] They add to the progressive tradition. The New Deal "for the first time in United States history," says C. Wright Mills, renders "social legislation and lower class issues...important features of the reform movement."[2] More than a century ago, social workers address urban poverty. However, turn of the twentieth century social workers draw from less powerful American political traditions then other contemporaneous progressive reformers and their opponents. From the late inception of the American republic, attempts to ameliorate poverty are not in themselves major parts of the then prevailing American attitude that informs interactions between the government and economy. Notwithstanding current misconceptions, during the United States' first few decades, those in business rarely if at all request laissez faire government. "The doctrine of 'laissez-faire,'" says Seymour Martin Lipset, "became dominant only after the growth of large corporations and private investment funds reduced the pressures for public funds."[3]

Pre-Jacksonian era Americans presume the workings of a closely intertwined government and private industry. Both Jeffersonians and Hamiltonians take for granted the necessity of government–business cooperation. Government and private industry alliances are indispensible for national development of commerce and infrastructure. Only government can then provide enough investment capital for industry to flourish. Virtually every early American believes that "private" corporations should benefit the public good while generating private wealth. America's proto-industrialists took pleasure in being aware of their civic responsibilities. "Convinced, on the whole, of an identity between moral and material progress, these industrialists, while not averse to profits," says Lipset, "were conscious of making a patriotic contribution and of trying to establish a pattern in manufacturing for the nation."[4]

Everyone considers these corporations both public and private ventures.[5] State and federal governments make this assumption. "For the first forty years of Pennsylvania's existence as a state within the Union, there was little argument over the propriety or even necessity of direct state participation in ownership as a means of facilitating economic development," says Lipset, describing Pennsylvania as a typical state. "Pennsylvania and other American states followed a policy of government investment in areas basic to economic growth where private efforts seemed inadequate."[6]

DOI: 10.1057/9781137527813.0011

Hamilton spearheads the interests of finance, commerce, and manufacturing. However, like the economic components Hamilton favors, early American agriculture requires government assistance in managing, regulating, and growing foreign exports and trade, expanding agricultural markets, handling the western territories, and developing new technologies, networks of commerce, roads, canals, and waterways.

Jefferson is more wary than Hamilton of the possible threats posed by the oligarchy and tyranny of a seemingly distant government. However, Jefferson is not a narrow ideologue. He advocates the funding of public schools through government taxation; famously uses the elastic clause of the Constitution (Article 1, section 8, Clause 18 granting Congress power "To make all Laws which shall be necessary and proper for carrying into Execution the foregoing Powers, and all other Powers vested by this Constitution in the Government of the United States, or in any Department or Officer thereof") to secure the Louisiana Purchase (though he had criticized Hamilton's use of the elastic clause to establish a national bank). As president, Jefferson comes to believe that the national government must help to establish a strong American manufacturing sector. Jefferson, says Lipset, "felt compelled, when President, to modify his former objections to manufacturing," maintaining that his views concerning manufacturing and cities apply to Europe and not the United States.[7] President Jefferson supports nascent American industry's growth.

Jefferson's economic struggle with Hamilton involves finance more than it does manufacturing. Jeffersonians are never "reconciled to banking and stockjobbing," notes Schlesinger, and this is their "abiding difference with the Hamiltonians."[8] This difference between Jefferson and Hamilton takes on a growing import in the 1830s when Andrew Jackson problematizes the practice of government financing private industry. Jackson argues against creating and reinforcing what Jackson perceives to be the anti-democratic power implicit in governmentally funding only some corporations.

However, in the 1830s, government and not business is in the forefront of articulating the problem of favoring some business ventures over others. "Could it really be urged that the framers of the constitution intended that our Government should become a government of brokers?" says Jackson. "If so, then the profits of this national brokers' shop must inure to the benefit of the whole and not a few privileged monied capitalists to the utter rejection of the many."[9]

DOI: 10.1057/9781137527813.0011

Jackson's primary stated intent in this regard is democratizing the American economy to its fullest extent by not using public finance to privilege particular private citizens and corporations. Arguably, Jackson's unstated interests might lie in favoring southern and western enterprises over those of the "eastern establishment" or in slowing manufacturing altogether. However, Jackson's purpose is certainly in accord with the age's momentum toward granting political equality and the voting franchise to all white men. Indeed, Jackson's own rationale for his actions garners Jackson great popularity.

According to C. Wright Mills, "The Jacksonian Revolution was much more of a status revolution than an economic or a political one."[10] From a social and political perspective, Jackson voices an opposition to the kind of patrician rule characterizing even founders like Jefferson. Ironically, the same populist democratic impulse causing Jackson to pull government back half a century later leads to government extending its hand in the form of anti-trust legislation. "Though Jacksonian slogans such as 'That government is best that governs least' were later used to resist government restrictions on business," says Henry L. Watson, "it is clear that they were not formulated for that purpose. Jackson wanted to keep government out of business in order to starve the 'monster' on its cradle [as Grover Norquist says of government a century and a half later], not to liberate it from democratic controls."[11]

In fact, a strong Jeffersonian such as James Madison, in the interests of human rights and the harmonious workings of the American government, parts with Jefferson's ideas about states' rights. Madison originally urges that the constitution should charge the federal government with the power to veto any state law in order to prevent "the aggressions of interested majorities on the rights of minorities and of individuals," in addition to preventing states from "harass[ing] each other with rival and spiteful measures dictated by mistaken views of interest."[12]

Jeffersonians and Hamiltonians alike see little problem in checking self-interest for the greater good. Indeed, under President Jefferson, Treasury Secretary Albert Gallatin proposes a comprehensive national plan for building waterways, canals, and roads. Gallatin believes "individual exertion" insufficient and "the General Government alone" capable of financing the project.[13] However, President Jackson's belief that government unjustly privileges the enterprises that it regulates and funds causes him to block cooperation between business and government and ultimately scuttle the Gallatin plan that John Quincy Adams wishes to

DOI: 10.1057/9781137527813.0011

implement. It is Jackson's government and not business that first objects to government overseeing private enterprise. The public works plan that Gallatin and John Quincy Adams prize does not fructify after Jackson vetoes an 1830 bill authorizing the federal government to purchase the stock of a corporation constructing a road through Kentucky.

This changes after the Civil War when private corporations no longer require government investment. In addition, issues concerning slavery, the Civil War, and reconstruction divert the focus of reformers and the nation. Civil War production expands the wealthy corporations' power and influence. Although large corporations would still avail themselves of public largess, wealthy industrialists officially profess the virtues of absolute government laissez faire.

However, the original and "default" American position of cooperation between government and business is not entirely forgotten. This mindset expresses itself in legislation such as the 1897 Interstate Commerce Act and the 1890 Sherman Anti-Trust Act. Indeed, late nineteenth and early twentieth century populism and progressivism are grounded in an early American tradition of the government's interaction with free enterprise.

During the 1830s, wealthy individuals associated with big corporations rarely advocate for a laissez faire government. Indeed, Jackson's inclination to separate government from business works against industry by delaying America's construction of the conditions that would have fostered more rapid national industrial growth. On February 2, 1837, John Quincy Adams voices his regret about not being able to foresee what America might have been like in 1847 if he had been reelected as the president in 1828. "With this system in ten years from this day, the structure of the whole Union would have been checkered over with railroads and canals," says Adams. "It may still be done half a century later and with the limping gait of State legislature and private adventure. I would have done it in the administration of the affairs of the nation." Adams bemoans Jackson's unfortunate meddling with what he views as the success of the original "American system," as Henry Clay termes it after the end of the War of 1812 makes it possible for the federal government to resume directly fostering economic growth.

Adams surmises that "I fell and with me fell, I fear never to rise again, the system of internal improvement by means of national energies."[14] He is somewhat prophetic. The ensuing Panic of 1837 probably is caused more by the Bank of England's raising of its interest rates than by any of the domestic economic policies followed by Andrew Jackson or Martin

DOI: 10.1057/9781137527813.0011

Van Buren, but Jackson's slowing of national expenditures upon his infrastructure and disrupting of the customary federal modes of financing private investments through banks exasperate the crisis and help to cause bank runs, widespread unemployment, and rioting.

The American money supply does not definitively recover until the 1848 discovery of gold in California. By that time American industry still courts government subsidies but does not absolutely rely on them. Only after the Civil War does full-blown laissez faire ideology become a dogma of wealthy Gilded Age industrialists who deny the initial American system of government and business cooperation.

Jackson is more suspicious of government favoritism than Jefferson and his allies had been. Although more devoted to democratic principles than Hamilton, Jefferson initially stresses local over central government primarily as a strategy to achieve a relatively democratic republican form of democracy. Jefferson's concept of a republican democracy dovetails with his patrician mindset which would moderate the interests of the American people through the self-evident wisdom of a benevolent elite. However, Jefferson's advocacy of free and "universal" white public education that includes women indicates that Jefferson sees the limits of patrician government.

Lipset's formulation of the United States as "the first new nation" is infused with ideas about "equality" as an animating principle resulting in the rejection of entrenched superiority and the extension of the voting franchise electing Jackson. "Equality," says Lipset, "was reflected in the introduction of universal [white male] suffrage in America long before it came in other nations; in the fairly consistent and extensive support for a public school system so that all [whites] might have a common educational background; and in the pervasive antagonism to domination by any elite in culture, politics, or economics."[15]

After all, says Lipset, "For people to be equal, they need a chance to become equal. Success, therefore, should be attainable by all, no matter what the accidents of birth, class, or race."[16] A national consensus grows around public education in post-Jacksonian America. The Whig Party, forming in opposition to Jackson, stresses public education as a major part of its platform, and Jacksonians though less enthusiastic also support public education.

And yet the wish to aid the poor is not a large part of this early American consensus tacitly asking government to watch over some aspects of the American life and economy. Assisting the poor, however,

DOI: 10.1057/9781137527813.0011

has some adherents. For instance, in 1857, historian and politician George Bancroft asserts: "Abandonment of labor to the unmitigated effects of personal competition can never be accepted as the rule for the dealings of man to man.... The good time is coming, when humanity will recognize all members of its family as alike entitled to its care; when the heartless jargon of overproduction in the midst of want will end in a better science of distribution."[17] Bancroft's advocacy for granting universal suffrage and expanding the opportunities available for Americans receiving a secondary education, in addition to his establishment of the US Naval Academy at Annapolis and the US Naval Observatory while serving as the US Secretary of the Navy from 1845 to 1846, speak to Bancroft's belief that the state is based on its people and its education.

However, Bancroft's underlying concept is to deal indirectly with poverty, without the targeted solutions social workers later posit. Similarly, Ralph Waldo Emerson's 1844 "The Young American" announces, "Government has been a fossil; it should be a plant.... We have feudal governments in a commercial age.... Government has other offices than those of banker and executioner." Emerson envisions an informal cultural mode of government in which those with an inherent leadership knack are organically recognized so they can fulfill their "duty to instruct the ignorant, to supply the poor with work and with good guidance."[18] Emerson also envisions mysterious and indirect solutions.

The distrust of government measures to spur the economy through direct assistance to the poor prevails before the New Deal, reflecting an entrenched American mindset. Even in the 1830s Tocqueville identifies a prevalent American "principle of self-interest"[19] that Arthur M. Schlesinger, Jr. later relates with a 1980s drive toward "privatization."[20] Emerson's 1848 view of socialism as a disincentive to "the motive of industry" "mak[ing] all men idle & immortal" and thus increasing the number of poor people who would become "a burden on the state" jibes with current American opposition to extremely light doses of "socialism" in the form of government job programs.[21]

Despite the later valorizing of New Deal job programs by many historians, intellectuals, and artists, such job programs were generally considered suspect during the New Deal. A Depression character in Harper Lee's *To Kill a Mockingbird* remarks, "If he held his mouth, Mr. Cunningham could get a WPA job, but his land would go to ruin if he left it, and he was willing to go hungry to keep his land and vote as he pleased."[22]

DOI: 10.1057/9781137527813.0011

As previously noted, people employed in New Deal work programs are officially considered unemployed in labor statistics. The 10% of the workforce at one point employed by the WPA are statistically considered unemployed.[23] This fact, in addition to stressing the temporary 1937 Roosevelt Recession brought about by FDR slashing the budget and cutting back on job programs, accounts for recent criticisms of the New Deal which maintain that the New Deal did not alleviate unemployment.

This American mindset dovetails with that of pre-industrial rural America. Industrialization and urbanization come later to the United States than to Great Britain and Europe. In America, immigrants with whom most Americans do not readily identify feel much of the Industrial Revolution's negative impact. In addition, nineteenth century America has the "safety-valve" of unsettled territories. All of these factors contribute to an American mindset that is relatively unaffected by poverty following in industrialization and urbanization's wake.

Before the prevalence of industry and the city, poverty is less noticeable and more difficult to define. "She is no use here. She's a peasant; she ought to be in the country," says Natasha in Anton Chekhov's *Three Sisters*.[24] If nature, for nineteenth century painters, furnishes an open-ended subject for the "sublime" that counteracts the ill effects of industry and city, for a character such as Natasha the countryside provides an open-ended location to jettison workers whom she deems useless. However, the Industrial Revolution codifies labor according to its usefulness and brings workers to cities where the unemployed and working poor are more noticeable. Cities make the poor visible. When this begins to occur in the United States, private social work efforts emerge. It is almost as if the poor now need to be "codified" within the nation's new industrialized terms.

If the New Deal did not change this narrative, it nonetheless offers a counter-narrative Americans never reconcile. A central area of contention is how to contextualize the poor. The need to put them in context does not arise until the Industrial Revolution leads to urbanization. However, since industrializing and a resulting urbanizing happens in the United States decades after they do in Great Britain and Europe, middle and upper class Americans are slower to account for any notion of poverty as a systemic economic problem that is not due to presupposed sloth, alcoholism, and other shortcomings of poor individuals themselves.

No figure so clearly bridges the gap between social work and government as Frances Perkins. Without looking through the historical lens

DOI: 10.1057/9781137527813.0011

that Perkins's work provides it is difficult to appreciate the New Deal's seismic effect on American life. Perkins's career morphs seamlessly from adventurous and professionally undefined turn of the century social work to achieving the ends of early social work through government. Her trailblazing work in the position of a semi-private, semi-government (the National Consumers League lends her to the New York State government) chief Triangle Shirtwaist Factory fire investigator is the tipping point between Perkins as a social worker and government administrator.

Before investigating the Triangle Fire, Perkins herself could not imagine the sea change that the role of government undergoes. Most Americans are now accustomed to the federal government claiming at least partial responsibility for their economic and social wellbeing. They look to the nation's government to provide social safety nets, such as old-age pensions and unemployment insurance. The federal government aids the disabled and helps to regulate child labor, the minimum wage, maximum workweek hours, and safe working conditions.

However, these federal government duties are relatively new concepts. An astonishing amount of the legal and governmental infrastructure corresponding to these ideas is established during Franklin Delano Roosevelt's New Deal, which is conceptualized by one key Roosevelt advisor. When Kirstin Downey calls Frances Perkins "the woman behind the New Deal," Downey means that Perkins is vital in formulating its goals, rationales, and methods of implementation.[25]

Perkins is the first Roosevelt advisor to propose with specificity the New Deal's social program.[26] Before agreeing to join his administration in February 1933, Perkins requires the President-elect to agree to support several progressive social work goals that she advocates. As her condition for agreeing to serve as FDR's Secretary of Labor, Roosevelt says that he will back Perkins's efforts to bring about unemployment insurance, worker's compensation, old-age pensions, a federal child labor ban, a forty-hour workweek, a minimum wage, public work programs, aid to the disabled, national health insurance, and an agency to help the unemployed find work.[27] Roosevelt and Perkins only fail to legislate national health insurance.

Perkins plays a prominent role in all of these achievements. She spearheads the drafting of the 1935 Social Security Bill and the 1938 Fair Labor Standards Act, reorganizes the US Department of Labor, soothes labor strife, and improves working conditions during the difficult periods of

DOI: 10.1057/9781137527813.0011

the Depression and World War II, in addition to administering many of the New Deal's key public work programs, labor relation boards, and domestic war programs.

Perkins, the fourth US Secretary of Labor, is the first female presidential cabinet member. She is also the first woman to head a New York State government department. However, the magnitude of these accomplishments at times obscures her importance in transforming American government. Perkins's brand of early twentieth century social work equips her with a set of goals and methods that contribute to this transformation. In 1910 Perkins begins working for the National Consumers' League, a position leading her to national renown for investigating the Triangle Shirtwaist Factory fire.

Although as both a social worker and a politician Perkins has practical aims, she also has a comprehensive social philosophy. Perkins aims to open the workplace to all Americans, making it a place of individual and collective learning and development. She envisions a nation without poverty where everyone would help to alleviate debilitating individual circumstances.[28] Although her vision is not fully enacted, she serves a government in which key aspects of it come to pass. Perkins helps articulate and oversee the overlapping imbrications of social work and government within the nation. "The welfare of the people" has only in the 1930s definitively become, to repeat Perkins's mission statement for the Democratic Party, "the first charge upon the government."[29]

The methods Perkins uses in fusing social work and government are difficult to delineate. However, several characteristic methods become clear when analyzing Perkins's careers within social work and government. These methods are derived from Perkins's social work experiences and are in themselves a part of social work's impact on government. Perkins's most important methodological contribution is that of the conference method. She also furthers Florence Kelley's investigatory and advocacy methods. The bold and persistent audacity with which she speedily utilizes unexpected resources is a mark of early social work and also of Perkins's manner of creative social casework prefiguring the New Deal. Perkins's pragmatism reflects the New Deal's propensity to adapt to realities to achieve New Deal goals. Her ability to gain the trust of important politicians with significant information reflects a more personal kind of Perkins method that is rooted in social work methodology. Perkins's social work skills blend into her groundbreaking governmental triumphs.

DOI: 10.1057/9781137527813.0011

Through government Perkins achieves many of the goals she holds as a social worker. However, Perkins herself sharply distinguishes government from social work when New York Governor Alfred E. Smith first asks her to join his Democratic administration in 1919. Like Roosevelt afterwards, Smith recruits Perkins and the social work programs she advocates as vital to the success of his administration. It is important to understand that social work is as much in demand by those in government and politics as social workers seek government's clout.

Perkins's advice to political operatives in 1936 demonstrates how preconceptions about the federal government change during the New Deal. A mindset emerges during the New Deal that supplants both conservative and earlier progressive attitudes, ideals, and ideas so that Perkins's social work career informs her work within government.

Frances Perkins is the first Roosevelt advisor to articulate the strategy underlying the 1936 FDR presidential reelection campaign. Since Perkins believes "the welfare of the people is the first charge upon the government," unlike other Democratic National Committee (DNC) advisors, Perkins tells the Democrats to "own" the emergency measures they have helped enact. However, a DNC strategist tells her they do not "make a good story."[30] "We haven't done anything startling," he tells Perkins when consulting her about the campaign's mission.[31]

It is difficult now to realize how radical Perkins's advice is. For instance, all through the 1930s work programs such as the Work Progress Administration are unpopular and considered fiscally wasteful boondoggles. Indeed, the term "boondoggle" refers to what Perkins calls a "cowboy" word for characteristic cowboy gadgets, accessories, and saddle trappings. When a Western WPA project proposes making "boondoggling" items, New Deal opponents uncritically deride the program solely due to this word. It is thus unsurprising that people who work for programs such as the WPA and the CCC are considered unemployed.

For most Americans before the New Deal, government suggests grand matters of state that proceed outwards from the government itself; Alexander Hamilton referred to these government actions as centrifugal. However social work implies aiding isolated individuals and families directly. These actions might be called centripetal. In the Depression social work becomes tantamount to helping the American people. However, the workings of the federal government in particular are not generally associated with social work. Perkins notes that before the New

DOI: 10.1057/9781137527813.0011

Deal, "There had never been any declaration by any great power that the promotion of the welfare of the working people was a high objective of the nation and its legislative policy."[32]

According to Perkins, a new relationship between Americans and their government "normalizes" and institutionalizes the emergency measures taken during the first years of the Roosevelt administration, bringing the aims of the federal government nearer to the aims Perkins's concept of social work embodies. Perkins is perhaps first to see how this shift "brands" the Democratic Party and to act on this insight.

It is telling that progressives of the "Progressive Era" of twenty to thirty years before the New Deal do not generally support the New Deal. After all, before the New Deal, progressives are skeptical of both big business and big government. However, those inspired by the goals of social work tend to value humanitarian results over considerations of political process. It is unsurprising that early social work progressives later form a core part of the New Deal's constituency. Even some centrifugal actions such as the TVA (Tennessee Valley Authority) are more governmentally positive than Progressive Era trust busting. In many respects the New Deal grows out of the early days of social work.

The 1936 election dramatically reformulates the relation between Americans and their government. Perkins figures prominently in centering FDR's campaign upon this reformulation. This new relationship between government and people brings the aims of the federal government closer to those Perkins's social work embodies.

In a sense, social work fills the void left by government's limited reaction to the social problems of the Industrial Revolution. "Social work," says Schlesinger, arises "in the late nineteenth century as [a] nonpolitical response" to the "miseries and injustices" caused by the industrialization of America.[33] A progressive Protestant "Social Gospel," declaring the upper and the middle classes responsible for the poor and the working classes, grows into volunteer social charity work by religious-based organizations such as the Methodist Federation for Social Services and the Federal Council of Churches.[34]

At the turn of the twentieth century, many progressives call for the federal government to address the lives of ordinary Americans. Their successes include the federal 1906 Pure Food and Drug Act that regulated food and medicine; the 1914 Federal Trade Commission Act to cope with large trusts and unfair trade practices; and constitutional amendments instituting a national income tax, direct elections of United

DOI: 10.1057/9781137527813.0011

States senators by the American people, and women's suffrage. However, progressivism becomes less popular during World War I and the 1920s. In that decade the nation elects three laissez faire Republican presidents whom big business prefers to Theodore Roosevelt and Woodrow Wilson.

Since Franklin Roosevelt is the first Democratic president after Wilson, it is sometimes assumed that the New Deal flows directly from the Progressive Era. However, the New Deal is not a mere offshoot of progressivism. Although the federal government assumes new responsibilities between the turn of the century and World War I, in the Progressive Era the federal government never functions as a social safety net for the poor, disabled, unemployed, or elderly. Otis L. Graham, Jr. points out that most of the progressives living to see the New Deal do not support it. Notable progressives such as Hiram Johnson, Walter Lippmann, Charles Evans Hughes, Edgar Lee Masters, Henry L. Stimson, Carter Glass, and William Allen White are a small sample of a surprisingly long list of prominently established progressives who oppose the New Deal.[35]

According to Graham, many progressives wish to "restore the small-town synthesis their fathers presumably enjoyed."[36] Progressive Era reforms such as establishing the Federal Trade Commission (FTC) and trust busting utilize government to fight big business and industry. However, most progressives do not identify with big government. Progressives tend to oppose "the power of the meddling state." They look critically at both big business and big government.

It is not surprising that many progressives are uncomfortable with the New Deal.[37] New Deal programs such as the National Recovery Act accept the status of big business and industry as instrumental to the nation's wellbeing. It might have then been expected therefore that progressives sitting on the Supreme Court such as Charles Evans Hughes and Louis Brandeis strike down the NRA as unconstitutional. As progressives, a distrust of both government and industrial "bigness" guides the two justices. Progressives, says Graham, "were less than enthusiastic over doing the right thing as part of some obedient mass and at the demand of some bureaucrat. Understandably, many of them found the 'conservative' side, the side of individualism and liberty, congenial in the 1930s."[38]

While most progressives are apprehensive about government's meddling, Perkins insists, "We must have the *courage* to meddle," and she wants government that does not fear to meddle when attempting to

DOI: 10.1057/9781137527813.0011

eradicate abject poverty.[39] The progressives most enthusiastic about the New Deal, as previously noted, are social workers preoccupied by social reform as is Frances Perkins.[40]

Lillian Wald, the founder of the Henry Street Settlement, says, "Franklin D. Roosevelt thinks as Lillian Wald and Jane Addams."[41] Reform-minded social workers, such as Paul Kellogg, are astounded that the New Deal's objectives are the same ones that they had had for thirty years: "public housing, relief, a minimum wage, an end to child labor, old-age security, maximum hours, and unemployment compensation."[42]

In many respects, the New Deal grows from the early days of social work. It borrows, says Graham, from those social workers with an "'anything can be done' spirit."[43] Franklin Roosevelt's inclination to try social experiments and remain steadfastly optimistic also owes much to the mindset of early social workers.[44] Perkins, says Downey, "shared the intense vitality that animated the Roosevelt family, the same intrinsic optimism, the same self-confidence bolstered by optimism."[45]

As previously noted Theodore Roosevelt's post-presidential support for early social workers and his correspondence with Perkins causes him to suggest her as the director of the first committee investigating the Triangle Fire, leading to her later placement within New York State government and her work with Al Smith and Franklin Roosevelt.[46] The New Deal echoes the result-oriented drive of the first decade of twentieth century social work.

However early social workers did not represent most surviving progressives or most Americans in general during the early 1930s. When the federal government assists everyday Americans at the start of the New Deal, the federal government's role as a social safety net seems temporary. Even Franklin Roosevelt does not view his emergency actions during the first years of his administration as having lasting consequences.[47]

"The 1936 campaign," says Perkins, "was a political education for the Democratic party."[48] Roosevelt's reelection is not the given that we might see it as today. That summer, a Democratic National Committee strategist working to reelect Roosevelt described the DNC's problem: "We haven't done anything startling, like setting up the Federal Reserve Banks, like Wilson did. What we've done doesn't make a good story."[49] It is difficult now to comprehend how the campaign strategist could *not* see New Deal programs, such as Social Security, as "a good story." Although many Americans now may not overly sympathize with the poor they tend to hold the federal government at least partially responsible for,

DOI: 10.1057/9781137527813.0011

as Perkins describes social work's aims, "making life better for ordinary people" who work.[50] Most Americans therefore now accept progressive social work's goals as those of their government.

"In 1946," Perkins writes, "it seems odd that none of us [before the New Deal] thought in terms of a federal law" to institute social reforms such as the regulation of child labor and the establishment of unemployment insurance.[51] "Labor and social legislation on a federal basis had been declared unconstitutional by the Supreme Court."[52] The US Supreme Court in 1918 and 1922 declares federal statutes regulating child labor unconstitutional.[53] Reformers in states such as Wisconsin and New York thought in terms of state rather than federal social reform.[54]

In the 1910s and 1920s, Perkins admits to thinking about social reform in New York more than in all of the United States. "I was much more aware of New York and of belonging to it than I was of belonging to the U.S.A., which perhaps is wrong and unpatriotic," she recalls.[55] "Before 1932," says Perkins, "no one in New York or New England, as far as I could discover, and I had lived there all my life, expected someone to come from Washington to solve a problem."[56] Before the New Deal, Western states sought federal aid and guidance, but their requests concerned natural resources more than social problems.[57]

If the Depression alters what Americans expect from the federal government, it is unclear how long this new expectation will last. At the start of his presidency, Roosevelt hesitates to launch most of the public work programs that others in his administration who are associated with social work urge. However, FDR eventually determines, "We have to do it. It is like putting all you've got into stopping up the hole in the dike."[58]

The New Deal, observes Perkins, grows from "necessary rescue actions" designed as stopgap measures against "the emergency" Roosevelt faces upon taking "office at the low point of the Depression."[59] Roosevelt is torn between the virtues of a balanced budget and public works relief programs viewed as "temporary emergency measures."[60] He knows that programs such as the Works Project Administration (WPA) will be thought of as "the dole." Indeed, the WPA is often incorrectly assumed to be corrupt and wasteful although, Schlesinger notes, New Deal programs undergo "much less graft ... than the conservative administrations of the 1920s." "Under FDR's New Deal," says Schlesinger, "the national government spent more money than ever before in peacetime and regulated the economy as never before; but there was a noticeable absence of corruption."[61] FDR scrupulously sets up New Deal programs to mitigate

DOI: 10.1057/9781137527813.0011

corruption. FDR is careful to separate the budget planning for New Deal programs from their administration. For instance, to Harold Ickes's chagrin, in 1935 Roosevelt asks Ickes to help oversee the WPA while Harry Hopkins plans and budgets it. Roosevelt knows any corruption can fatally wound work relief programs and the WPA requires Ickes's tough management style. However, in terms of planning, Ickes's frugality would be counterproductive to the New Deal's compensatory spending goals (by 1935 FDR is able to consider the virtue of compensatory spending), for which FDR knows Harry Hopkins is better suited. Nonetheless, the 1936 Roosevelt campaign avoids mentioning work programs such as the now celebrated WPA, PWA, and CCC.[62]

The 1935 Social Security Act establishes the enduring framework for many federal safety nets but its effect on the 1936 election is uncertain. The first old-age pension checks will not be distributed until 1940, making the act more vulnerable to being characterized in the 1936 campaign as a useless tax, an inefficient boondoggle, and an invasion of privacy. In addition, it is then not known if the Supreme Court will uphold the Social Security Act as constitutional. In fact, a major reason for the Democrats' "difficult political situation," according to Perkins, is the Supreme Court's rejection of two popular early New Deal programs, the Agricultural Adjustment Administration (AAA) and the National Recovery Administration.[63] The AAA improves the devastated rural economy, and many industrial workers think of the NRA as the New Deal itself. What has the present administration done of enduring value? Does it accomplish anything resembling the enduring achievement of "setting up the Federal Reserve Banks" or "reciprocal trade treaties"?

Perkins is "called in to help draft" "a campaign book, which," Perkins explains, "is a pamphlet that can be given to all speakers, all district leaders, all state chairman, all local chairmen, all subcommittees." This book provides "a record of what your party has done for its country, and then general outline of what we are claiming are the particular reasons why the Democratic party should be returned to power at this time."[64]

"Somebody suggested that I get you to come over and talk about this with me and two or three of us," a perplexed DNC aide tells Perkins:[65] "We're stuck on this business of getting up this campaign book. What are we going to say? The depression isn't over. We don't dare say we've healed the depression. All the economists and all these figures say that it's not over. It's better, but it isn't over." According to the strategists, unfortunately for the campaign, the present administration is not responsible for "the reciprocal trade treaties" and could not take credit for them.[66]

"The Democratic Party," responds Perkins, "has established the idea that the welfare of the people is the first charge upon the government."[67] Perkins's sense of what is politically apparent differs from the others at the DNC. "I can't imagine what the problem is," she says. "Look what we've done." She ticks off what the administration did, emphasizing "relief" to those in immediate need, public work programs, homeowner loans, aid to farmers, the government's role in spurring production and improving working conditions through the NRA, unemployment insurance, government assistance in finding jobs, and "saving the pride" of workers: "I went over and said, 'I can't imagine what the problem is. Look what we've done.'... We began with relief because the people were suffering.... relief to the veterans who converged on Washington.... we gave people quick cash relief. We got work relief...Home Owners Loan to save people's houses. What was that for? For nothing in the world except to save the homes of people. Then...farm mortgage legislation....We moved on to the public works jobs. We set up the NRA, which gave us a shot in the arm and established a floor under wages and a ceiling over hours. The country rejoiced. Thousands went back to work on that plan...we developed the WPA which was saving the pride of the little men, as well as of the professionals and laboring men. We had just then put through this great program of unemployment insurance. We established free public employment offices. We set up old-age insurance...I think there were some eighteen or twenty items. The whole purpose of everything we had done had been to bring healing and help to the common people, the people who were down and out."[68]

Perkins does not single out the Roosevelt administration's bank and financial reforms, and she also does not specifically mention many "items" she plays a role in accomplishing, such as helping to administer the popular Civilian Conservation Corp which employs more than three million young people and veterans to do environmental work of long-lasting value and smoothing the many instances of labor unrest that she is instrumental in calming and at times resolving.[69]

As a social worker, Perkins recognizes the political value of bringing "healing and help to the common people, the people who were down and out." The administration, according to Perkins, acts "out of sheer humanitarianism and because nobody could think of anything else to do."[70] Therefore, "this had not been evaluated by the politicians as

DOI: 10.1057/9781137527813.0011

politically important. In fact, they didn't think it was. It didn't occur to them."[71]

However, the New Deal's accomplishments thrill Perkins as a social worker, and she thinks most Americans feel similarly. After all, the administration responds to the self-evident economic and social needs of the American people, which is precisely what social work concerns. In a sense, it is difficult to single out what the New Deal does because what it does is so prevalent and potentially empowering for Americans. Perkins's novel formulation of the administration's chief accomplishment as "establish[ing] ... that the welfare of the people is" the government's first responsibility means that the administration cares about Americans, and Perkins assumes that Americans want a humane government responsive to their needs and directly engaging the nation's social and economic welfare—a government that in effect does social work on a large scale.

When Perkins explains her political assessment to the DNC's leaders, it surprises Roosevelt's campaign manager, James Farley, who asks her to "write that out, only fix it so that it could be said by anybody and let me circulate that. That's a good model for these boys to talk on."[72] The DNC writes Perkins's talking points "into the campaign book" and "when the campaign got going every speaker, including Joe Robinson, John Nance Garner, Alben Barkley, Pat Karrison, spoke out of this campaign book, saying, 'We did this, this and this.' "[73] Unlike in many recent elections, particularly in non-presidential Congressional election years, Democrats *own* their party's accomplishments.

Jim Farley later learns that Perkins's model for a new politics based on addressing the people's wellbeing, the animating aim of social work, is more than politically viable. "In the course of the campaign," remarks Perkins, "Jim remarked on how well it was going, and on the fine speech that someone had made on the basis of the model I had drawn up. He said, 'The response is wonderful. We did all these things out of just sheer goodness, you know, just decency. What could you do with everybody down and out, but that? You know, they're just discovering that there were votes in them thar hills.' "[74]

Perkins's rationale for reelection is extremely popular and results in a 1936 Democratic Party landslide that is the most one-sided presidential victory since George Washington's in 1792. "The politicians never realized that before until they came to campaign in '36," says Perkins: "That was what they had to say to the people. There wasn't anything else to say. They discovered, of course, to their astonishment, when the vote came

DOI: 10.1057/9781137527813.0011

in that there were votes, innumerable votes, in 'them thar hills.' It was just terrific."[75] Government actions addressing the social and economic welfare of individual Americans had shifted from being deemed politically insignificant to being "things [done] out of just sheer goodness, you know, just decency" to being acts of paramount political import.

If Perkins is instrumental in incorporating social welfare into the fundamental aims of American government, she also plays a central role in articulating that change. Perkins melds the relatively new science of social work into the art of politics. However, her entry into politics could not have been foreseen. Frances Perkins begins as a social worker. It is necessary to understand Perkins's career as a social worker to understand the change to come in America and government.

Notes

1   Schlesinger, vol. II, p. 299.
2   C. Wright Mills, *The Power Elite* (New York: Oxford University Press, 1956), p. 273.
3   Seymour Martin Lipset, *The First New Nation: The United States in Historical and Comparative Perspective* (New York: Basic Books, 1963), p. 52.
4   Ibid., pp. 57–58.
5   See Arthur M. Schlesinger, Jr., "Affirmative Government and the American Economy," *The Cycles of American Politics* (Boston: Houghton Mifflin Company, 1986), pp. 219–255.
6   Lipset, p. 52.
7   Ibid., p. 47.
8   Schlesinger, *Cycles of American Politics*, p. 221.
9   Quoted in Richard Hofstadter, *The American Political Tradition and the Men Who Made It* (New York: Vintage, 1989), p. 57.
10   Mills, p. 271.
11   Henry L. Watson *Liberty and Power* (New York: Hill and Wang, 1990), p. 171.
12   Madison to Washington, April 16, 1787, in James Madison *The Complete Madison: His Basic Writings*, ed. Saul K. Padover (New York, 1953), p. 185.
13   Albert Gallatin, "Report on Roads and Canals," in Carter Goodrich and Bobbs Merrill (ed.), *The Government and the Economy: 1783–1861* (Indianapolis, 1967), pp. 6–7.
14   John Quincy Adams to C.W. Upham, February 2, 1837, in Brook Adams, "A Compilation of the Message of the Presidents," Forgotten Books. *1789, 1897 U.S. Government Printing Office* (Washington: D.C, 1898), p. 258. Heritage

DOI: 10.1057/9781137527813.0011

of Henry Adams, "introduction to Henry Adams", *The Degradation of the Democratic Dogma* (New York, 1919), p. 25.

15 Lipset, p. 2.

16 Ibid.

17 George Bancroft, *The Necessity, The Reality, and the Promise of the Progress of the Human Race* (Nabu Press, 2012), p. 34.

18 Ralph Waldo Emerson, "The Young American," http://www.emersoncentral.com/youngam.htm

19 Alexis de Tocqueville, *Democracy in America*, volume II, third Book, chapter xxi.

20 Schlesinger, *Cycles of American Politics*, p. 42.

21 Ralph Waldo Emerson, *The Journals and Miscellaneous Notebooks of Ralph Waldo Emerson*, 16 volumes, eds. William H. Gilman and Ralph H. Orth, et al. (Cambridge, MA: Harvard University Press, 1960–1982), volume 10, p. 312.

22 Harper Lee, *To Kill a Mocking Bird* (New York: Harper Collins, 2006), p. 23.

23 Paul Krugman, *End This Depression Now* (New York: W.N. Norton & Company, 2013), p. 121.

24 Anton Chekhov, *The Three Sisters*, trans. Constance Garnett (New York: Macmillan, 1916), http://www.eldritchpress.org/ac/sisters.htm#act3

25 Downey, p. 1.

26 Ibid., pp. 1–3.

27 Ibid.

28 Perkins, "Helping."

29 Columbia University Libraries , Part 7, pp. 11–14.

30 Ibid., p. 11.

31 Ibid.

32 Perkins, *Roosevelt*, p. 338.

33 Schlesinger, vol. I, pp. 22–23.

34 Ibid.

35 Graham, pp. 192–193.

36 Ibid., p. 181.

37 Ibid., pp. 178–181.

38 Ibid., p. 177.

39 Coleman, p. 27.

40 Ibid., pp. 108–109.

41 Graham, pp. 109.

42 Ibid.

43 Ibid.

44 Ibid., p. 171.

45 Downey, p. 49.

46 Ibid., p. 47–49.

47 Perkins, *Roosevelt*, pp. 173–175.

48 Ibid., p. 121.

DOI: 10.1057/9781137527813.0011

49   Columbia University Libraries, Part 7, p. 11.
50   Perkins, *Roosevelt*, p. 167.
51   Ibid., p. 103.
52   Ibid., p. 104.
53   George Martin, *Madam Secretary: Frances Perkins* (Boston: Houghton Mifflin, 1976), pp. 218, 187
54   Perkins, *Roosevelt*, pp. 103–104.
55   Martin, p. 164.
56   Perkins, *Roosevelt*, pp. 169–170.
57   Ibid., p. 169.
58   Ibid., p. 175.
59   Ibid., p. 173.
60   Ibid., p. 175.
61   Schlesinger, *Cycles of American Politics*, p. 41.
62   Perkins, *Roosevelt*, p. 188.
63   Ibid., p. 121.
64   Columbia University Libraries, Part 7, p. 10.
65   Ibid., p. 11.
66   Ibid., p. 10.
67   Ibid., pp. 11–14.
68   Ibid., p. 14.
69   Jean Edward Smith, *FDR* (New York: Random House, 2007), pp. 319–322.
70   Columbia University Libraries, Part 7, p. 14.
71   Ibid., pp. 11–12.
72   Ibid., p. 13.
73   Ibid., pp. 12–13.
74   Ibid., pp. 13–14.
75   Ibid.

DOI: 10.1057/9781137527813.0011

9

Between Social Work and Government: Investigating the Triangle Fire and Perkins's Conference Method

Abstract: *This chapter concerns perhaps Frances Perkins's most celebrated "case": the Triangle Shirtwaist Factory fire. Perkins, with Al Smith's help, manages to open this "case" to a plethora of other dangerous and unhealthy workplace conditions for the New York State Factory Investigating Commission to explore. Tammany thus gives Perkins a grand opportunity to demonstrate to government officials the value of her conference method, setting the stage for entry into New York State government.*

Keywords: Al Smith; Bureau of Labor Statistics; New York State Factory Investigating Commission; Triangle Shirtwaist Factory fire

Miller, Stephen Paul. *The New Deal as a Triumph of Social Work: Frances Perkins and the Confluence of Early Twentieth Century Social Work with Mid-Twentieth Century Politics and Government.* New York: Palgrave Macmillan, 2016. DOI: 10.1057/9781137527813.0012.

The Triangle Fire investigation bridges Perkins's social work and government careers. She sees the fire on Saturday, March 25, 1911 while having tea at a friend's house on the north side of Washington Square Park. "People had just begun to jump as we got there," says Perkins.[1] Onlookers scream "Don't Jump. Help is on the way." However, because of the fire prevention expertise she acquires at the Consumers League, Perkins knows the fire department's ladders cannot reach the stranded workers and the firemen can do little.[2]

Before the Triangle Fire, Perkins investigates and researches fire safety issues for the Consumers League. She investigates the Newark, New Jersey 1910 Wolf Muslin Undergarment Company in which twenty-six workers die, and she warns that the New York area is awash in firetraps. After the 1911 Triangle Fire claims 146 victims and popular outrage erupts because of locked exit doors and other dangerous circumstances, Perkins's expertise in fire prevention is in demand.[3]

The Committee on Public Safety is formed in the immediate aftermath of the Triangle catastrophe. In June 1911, when former president Theodore Roosevelt is asked to chair the committee he suggests Perkins as its executive director instead. Roosevelt has been corresponding with Perkins about social reform issues.[4]

The privately funded committee lobbies Governor Dix to appoint a governmental investigative body to prevent future disasters. However, the Committee on Public Safety does not wish "the hand of politics" to compromise the investigation.[5] They do not trust the Tammany leaders. After all, one of the factors angering New York's working class is that some of the 146 Triangle Fire victims had struck in 1909 in the shirtwaist workers' strike, and Tammany-controlled police had helped suppress that strike.[6]

There is no indication that anything has changed since then. The Committee on Public Safety does not want politicians on the committee. However, Smith tells Perkins the state investigative body needs to combine state legislators and social workers. Perkins is at first reluctant to work on the New York State Factory Investigating Commission. She has difficulty imagining social workers and politicians sharing common cause and working so closely together, and she thinks Smith's notion "absurd" although later she calls it "the most useful piece of advice, I guess, we've ever had."[7]

Since Perkins initially thinks it would be a conflict of interest compromising her social work principles to investigate the 1911 Triangle Fire

DOI: 10.1057/9781137527813.0012

for New York State with Tammany politicians, she has the Consumers League "loan" her to the investigation and Perkins only has a "quasi-public office."[8] Perkins would prefer serving with progressive luminaries similar to those on the private Committee on Public Safety.[9]

However Al Smith envisions Perkins's social work skills and goals as valuable to the government and to Democratic Party politics. Smith also believes politics to be essential for Perkins to achieve her own social work goals. Tammany leadership backs Smith in enlisting Perkins to help with their "social work" strategy.

Although Tammany might seemingly ignore and outlast New Yorkers' outrage about the Triangle Fire, circumstances have changed since the 1909 shirtwaist workers strike. In 1910 Democrats win control of the New York State government for the first time in decades, and in 1911 Tammany needs a compelling reason to maintain control of the state, a rationale for its reelection and return to power. Murphy, Smith, and Wagner are certain that the Triangle Fire is the "right vehicle" to redefine the Democratic Party in New York State.[10]

Investigating the fire also suits Murphy's desire for a platform from which to run a Tammany politician for national office. Murphy, long frustrated in his attempts to elect a Tammany politician as New York governor, dreams of "one of his boys" having the base of a statewide elected office from which he could be elected president.[11] Murphy arranges for the 1924 Democratic National Convention to take place in New York to boost Smith's presidential candidacy but Murphy dies after a heart attack in April 1924, and he does not live long enough to see Smith win the 1928 Democratic nomination.[12]

Working with Perkins and other social workers like Belle Moskowitz, whom Perkins introduces to Smith, attunes Smith to new possibilities about what social reform offers voters. Moskowitz becomes a leading Smith advisor. (When FDR becomes governor in 1929, Smith demands he hire Moskowitz as his chief of staff. However, Roosevelt discovers that Perkins introduced Smith to Moskowitz, and the new governor prefers Perkins as a key social worker over Moskowitz.).

Ironically, just as the Progressive Era is ending and that era's social workers seem old-fashioned to the next social work generation, progressive social work is becoming instrumental to a state government in search of a reason to govern.

Smith is eager to investigate the Triangle Fire with Perkins in order to appeal to important electoral constituencies. He realizes that responding

DOI: 10.1057/9781137527813.0012

to the fire appropriately will endear the Democrats to new immigrants who feel unconnected with Tammany politicians. After all, many Jews and Italian Americans work in the garment industry, as do many women who soon will get the vote, which is won with Tammany's support in New York State, two years before the entire nation.

In 1911, Jewish, Italian American, and other ethnic voters who identify with those who die in the Triangle Fire, believe the victims could have been saved by better working conditions and sensible fire prevention measures. It seems as if it should have been illegal to lock exit doors, block access to elevators and stairs, not dispose regularly of flammable material, and have only one sagging fire escape that collapses.[13] "It is dawning on these thousands on thousands that such things do not have to be!" says Martha Bruere about a protest march that takes six hours to pass by her Fifth Avenue window.[14] A sense that it is possible to address long established social ills matches Perkins's lifelong optimism.

Forming the Factory Investigating Commission is a political risk since it might alienate some of Tammany's key contributors, but it seems worth that risk because without it Democrats have less reason to remain in office. It is important to recall that New York Republicans also court the working class vote. Interestingly, much as twenty-first century national health care reform adapts a Republican concept of reform that Republicans later renounce, Perkins and FDR adapt an early 1920s New York Republican concept, which Republicans later reject, of worker compensation as a state managed insurance plan. FDR will of course later call on Perkins to use this mechanism as a major component of unemployment and old-age insurance in the 1935 Social Security Act.

Even in New York City, Tammany's survival is at stake. Smith feels no choice but to organize a vigorous, professional, and enlightening investigation. And for this Smith feels he needs Perkins. When Perkins finally meets Murphy he asks if she is the "girl" who "beat him on the Fifty-Four Hour Bill." When she answers in the affirmative, he says that losing to her gained him votes.

Perkins relishes the opportunity to show the public and politicians the decrepit conditions of lower-class working conditions. She prides herself on showing Wagner and Smith the face of poverty and wishes Franklin Roosevelt had still been a state senator so that she could also show him. At an upstate factory, Perkins recounts, "We made sure Robert Wagner personally crawled through the tiny hole in the wall that gave exit to a

DOI: 10.1057/9781137527813.0012

step ladder covered with ice and ending twelve feet from the ground, which was euphemistically labeled 'Fire Escape.' "[15]

The Factory Investigating Commission (FIC) is a "new mode of government agency."[16] The New York State Factory Investigating Commission is specifically charged with powers tailored to enact legislation. The committee is given subpoena power and is able to propose New York State legislation. In addition, Smith expands the commission's reach to examine other workplace hazards including chemical dangers, which Perkins believes cause more fatalities than fires.

The resulting state bills that Perkins helps the FIC draft and lobby through to passage not only creates effective fire regulations that still form the basis for New York fire codes, but also establishes a model upon which city and state fire codes all over the country and the world are based. Perkins personally leads the commission in deriving fire and workshop safety codes that still form the basis for regulatory measures throughout the nation and the world.[17] The basis of these laws remains functional in New York and throughout America and the world one hundred years later.[18]

The state legislature passes eight of the commission's bills in 1913. These laws address the causes of the Triangle Fire. Doors must be unlocked and open outwards.[19] Tall buildings require automatic sprinkler systems, working fire escapes, and adequate exits. Factories need regular fire drills and a ban on smoking.[20] Flammable waste management and gas jet safety mechanisms become law. Taking home factory work is made illegal. Frequent inspections are instituted and guaranteed by reorganizing the State Department of Labor.[21] All state factories need to be registered with the Department.[22]

In the commission's second year, numerous commission bills become law. Factory overcrowding is outlawed. Fire-insulated enclosed staircases and more fire escapes are also mandated.[23] These laws also have a great bearing on workplace conditions beyond fire prevention. Factories need to provide clean and drinkable water, washing facilities, and sanitary and well-ventilated bathrooms. Child workers need proof of being over fourteen years old.[24]

All manner of civic groups, experts, and workers help the EIC accomplish this. Many testify. Commissioners investigate 3,385 worklaces including fifty plants, hear 472 witnesses contained in 7,000 pages of testimony, and conduct fifty-nine public hearings throughout the State.[25] Perkins believes fact-finding and the dissemination of information

DOI: 10.1057/9781137527813.0012

essential to social work. For the public's edification, safe and unsafe factories are compared. Public hearings give voice to oppressed workers. In their presence, employers cannot deny the realities of dire working conditions. Among its many achievements, the commission recommends and passes through legislature a law instituting a six-day ten-hour-day work limit.[26] Perkins believes the Triangle Fire victims did not die in vain.

"One of the great failings of many progressives was that they disdained practical politics," observes Von Drehle. However, Perkins is intensely dedicated to and inspired by the most minute and practical aspects of her work. "I am not afraid to put my hand into the dirt...to do the petty, unpleasant jobs."[27] Perkins has a great respect for data, and would comment that there is rarely any argument amongst engineers because, "If the weight that has to be supported by a pillar is greater than the pillar's strength to maintain it, they do not dispute with the pillar, they do something about it."[28] Perkins's respect for hard facts is reflected in her revamping of the Bureau of Labor Statistics (BLS) into the purveyor of reliable, objective data that it remains.

Perkins maintains the Triangle Fire changes America and creates a context for the reforms that follow.[29] Perkins uses the then novel power of large public hearings and conferences to accomplish reform. The popularity of the FIC's objective recommendations leads to a Tammany landslide in the 1913 New York elections. This causes Tammany Hall to rely on Perkins to advocate the passage of more progressive legislation such as a groundbreaking minimum wage law, additional labor reform laws, a women's voting rights law preceding the US Constitutional amendment extending the voting franchise to women, and a reorganization of state government more effectively to enforce these laws.[30] A few years later, in the wake of FIC's influence, a New York worker's compensation law follows.

After her FIC experience, Perkins's conference method takes center stage and proves effective in educating the public and marshalling public support. Perkins calls what is accomplished through the FIC a "turning point" in America. "The extent to which this legislation in New York marked a change in American political attitudes and policies toward social responsibility can scarcely be overrated," observes Perkins. "It was, I am convinced, a turning point; it was not only successful in effecting practical remedies but, surprisingly, it proved to be successful also in vote-getting."[31]

DOI: 10.1057/9781137527813.0012

Perkins dates the great era of America's modernization back to 1910, which though a year before the Triangle Fire nonetheless reflects Perkins's prior research and investigation concerning fire control and workplace safety. "I sometimes pinch myself," says Perkins, "at realizing how far we came in making America modern in the years 1910–1940."[32]

Christopher N. Breiseth, who "invites Frances Perkins to live with us at our student residence at Cornell University, where she had come to teach in 1955 in the School of Industrial and Labor Relations," maintains that Perkins "observed that the New Deal began on March 25th, 1911," the day of the Triangle Fire.[33] Perkins believes that the goal of the committees investigating the fire is to resign themselves to vanishing, but only after integrating its manner of working into government. "Once these methods were established," says Perkins, "once the public was cooperative, and once the scientific and other agencies that know about these matters were cooperating to the limit, there was less and less [for the committee] to do. It took care of itself automatically."[34]

Perkins's formulation of what she would later term "the conference method" begins when she is a social work volunteer at Hull House from 1904 to 1907. In 1943 Perkins says Jane Addams "taught us to take all elements of the community into conference for the solution of any human problem."[35]

Meredith A. Newman notes that Perkins is "decades ahead of her time in her advocacy of the conference method to reach consensus over seemingly intractable problems."[36] Although Perkins's development of the conference method is an outgrowth of Perkins's training in social work, Perkins uses the conference method to find solutions through government.

Perkins believes that for a government properly to function the conference method is essential. She feels government should be more than a "cop." "An intelligent relationship between government and industry, one which naturally presupposes understanding and integrity on both sides, can result from the cooperative, or conference, method of industrial relation," says Perkins. "The conference method means, first of all, the establishment of professional standards in industrial management. A non-ethical industry is as dangerous to the community as a non-ethical doctor. When government substitutes conference and voluntary agreement for the big stick," Perkins explains, "one of the first gains is in giving that enlightened group a chance to set standards for the whole industry."[37]

DOI: 10.1057/9781137527813.0012

The conference method specifically involves getting all of an issue's relevant parties into a discussion, with each party presenting information and perspectives. Although this approach now seems common, the idea is innovative at the time. "Perkins's method to promote reform, first fully developed with the FIC, but then employed throughout the rest of her career, was to assemble a group of intelligent people," notes Christopher N. Breiseth, "including key public officials and others with technical expertise for the problem being addressed, then carrying out research to establish the facts of the situation before reaching conclusions and shaping the group's recommendations."[38] When Perkins later says that fifty intelligent and committed people can change the world she is not exaggerating.[39] She believes the Factory Investigating Commission does this through the conference method. However, the FIC's success also requires the legislative might of Smith and Wagner. Through government, social work succeeds collectively. Through social work, New York government remakes itself.

Notes

1   Von Drehle, p. 194.
2   Ibid., p. 195.
3   Ibid., pp. 214–215.
4   Downey, pp. 48–49.
5   Von Drehle, pp. 208–209.
6   Ibid., p. 213.
7   Ibid., p. 210.
8   Martin, p. 101.
9   Von Drehle, pp. 208–209.
10 Ibid., p. 211.
11 Ibid., p. 262.
12 Martin, pp. 182–183.
13 Downey, p. 51.
14 US Department of Labor, "The New York Factory Investigating Commission," http://www.dol.gov/oasam/programs/history/mono-regsafepart07.htm
15 Von Drehle, p. 215.
16 Downey, p. 50.
17 Ibid., pp. 52–53.
18 Ibid., p. 53.
19 Von Drehle, p. 215.

DOI: 10.1057/9781137527813.0012

20   Perkins, *Roosevelt*, pp. 23–24.
21   Von Drehle, p. 215.
22   Martin, p. 109.
23   Ibid., p. 108.
24   Downey, pp. 51–53.
25   US Department of Labor.
26   Martin, p. 113.
27   Von Drehle, p. 215.
28   Frances Perkins, "A Cooperative Program Needed for Industrial Stabilization," *Annals of the American Academy of Political and Social Science*, 154 (March 1931): 126.
29   Martin, p. 120.
30   Von Drehle, pp. 217–218.
31   Perkins, *Roosevelt*, p. 23.
32   Ibid., p. 108.
33   Christopher N. Breiseth, "From the Triangle Fire to the New Deal: Frances Perkins in Action," Talk given at the New York State Museum, Albany, New York, March 25, 2011, http://francesperkinscenter.org/docs/Breiseth-TRIANGLE-FIRE-TO-NEW-DEAL.pdf
34   Columbia University Libraries, Part 1, p. 387.
35   Newman, p. 84.
36   Ibid., p. 84.
37   Perkins, "Helping," p. 624.
38   Breiseth.
39   Columbia University Libraries, Part 1, p. 168.

DOI: 10.1057/9781137527813.0012

10

Social Work through Government

Abstract: *This chapter follows Perkins's adaption of social work through government. The chapter spotlights how Perkins becomes a Democrat; her settling of the Rome copper strike; her becoming the chief New York State Industrial Commissioner; her promoting of the US Labor Department "employment agency" hiring for the CCC and WPA; her crafting of the Social Security Act, Wagner Act, and Fair Labor Standards Act; her initiating of the Bureau of Labor Statistics as a keeper of credible statistics; and her helping to maintain adequate working standards during World War II.*

Keywords: Consumer Price Index; eight-hour workday; individual and collective rights; National Recovery Administration; National War Labor Board; personal; Rosie the Riveter

Miller, Stephen Paul. *The New Deal as a Triumph of Social Work: Frances Perkins and the Confluence of Early Twentieth Century Social Work with Mid-Twentieth Century Politics and Government*. New York: Palgrave Macmillan, 2016.
DOI: 10.1057/9781137527813.0013.

DOI: 10.1057/9781137527813.0013

Governor Al Smith intentionally merges social work and government. "If we're to get good government," says Smith, "there'd better not be any separation between social workers and the government."[1] After Perkins introduces Smith to social worker Belle Moskowitz, Moskowitz becomes the governor's most influential advisor. Social work folds into government. The alliances that social workers forge with Democratic politicians are largely responsible for keeping social reform an active force within New York State during the nationwide politically reactionary 1920s. New York stands virtually alone, with some competition from Wisconsin, as a post-World War I bastion of legislative social experimentation. New York's openness to social reform creates a direct line from advances made in the wake of the Triangle Fire investigation straight through to the New Deal. It is only due to the political success of the programs that Perkins and other social workers help enact into law that Governor Smith can fly in the face of the national conservative trend and further a progressive agenda. FDR calls what Perkins and Smith do in New York, starting with the Factory Investigating Commission, the New Deal's core.[2]

Al Smith's election as governor in 1918 testifies to the success of Tammany's social work agenda, and it makes sense for Smith to select Perkins as a member of the Industrial Commission, which governs the New York Department of Labor.[3] However, Perkins is surprised by Smith's plan to appoint her as a member of the New York Industrial Commission, which is part of the Department of Labor's reorganization. Such a high appointment for a woman in New York is unprecedented and "startling."[4] Perkins believes Kelley will find "a great distinction between people who work for the Consumers League, who work for social betterment, and mere political administration." However, Smith counters Perkins's apprehension: "If you girls are going to get what you want through legislation, there'd better not be any separation between social workers and the government."[5]

Perkins wants to stay out of government and avoid "political commitments" and the need "to protect anybody." She prefers being able to "speak out openly."[6] However, Florence Kelley, who had served in Illinois government with less impact than Perkins will, upsets Perkins's preconceived notions of how Kelley will view her possible appointment. Kelley convinces Perkins that "millions of working girls...should be represented by at least one woman."[7]

Although Perkins campaigns for Smith in 1918, she is not a registered Democrat. Smith persuades her that to accomplish her social reform

DOI: 10.1057/9781137527813.0013

aims she needs to work within the stability of the two-party system. "If you don't have a party organization, you won't continue to have a two-party system of government. If you don't have that, you'll have a kind of bedlam" and, says Smith, there will be no "progress."[8] Without a party organization, Smith tells Perkins, people in privileged positions will simply nominate themselves for office.

Even if moneyed interests are also in the Democratic Party, Smith continues, Perkins's social reform allies can overcome them. Smith uses the example of how she overcame Murphy and Huyler's opposition to pass the Fifty-Four-Hour Bill. His arguments convince Perkins that she can accomplish her social work goals through the "instrument" of the Democratic Party.[9]

Perkins's social work methodology in addition to her social work goals contributes to Smith's nomination of Perkins. Her success in applying the conference method to investigate the Triangle Fire forecasts how Perkins will jumpstart the New York State Industrial Commission to meet regularly and with a greater sense of purpose. When she starts as commissioner, Perkins says the commission "hardly functioned."[10] She therefore conferences with the entire commission staff, including its factory inspectors, and analyzes all work, eventually creating a more productive atmosphere.

Perkins has previously been extremely critical of the other industrial commissioners for disregarding the FIC's fire prevention recommendations and allowing a fire to occur in a Brooklyn candy factory, the temperatures at which sugar is boiled making candy factories particularly prone to fire. After the fire, she publicly speculates that the commissioners might be criminally negligent. Nonetheless, a friend advises Perkins to pretend she never criticized the other commissioners, and this strategy works.

Perkins overcomes conflicts of interest and corruption within the Industrial Commission's workmen's compensation committee, and she schedules regular and productive weekly conferences. Perkins befriends fellow commissioners, whom she once publicly said should be removed. To win their cooperation, she never acts alone and always requests the advice of other commissioners.[11] "Conferencing" values informing the conference method are crucial in Perkins's success in her government job. As a demonstration of Perkins's social work-related ability to inspire confidence, although her fellow commission members are initially unfriendly to her, she soon is virtually running the commission.[12]

DOI: 10.1057/9781137527813.0013

Perkins is instrumental in getting the Industrial Commission to tackle difficult labor situations such as the violent copper workers' strike in Rome, New York. In 1919 Perkins is able to convene the entire commission at the site of a violent labor dispute. Th at meeting occurs after Perkins drives into the midst of the bedlam of a copper workers' strike in Rome, New York, and through discussion Perkins pacifies about twenty men who meet her car armed with rocks. Using her social work skills to gain the strikers' confidence, they let her in on their plans to use dynamite they have stockpiled. Governor Smith has already sent state police to counter the strikers, and she fears a confrontation between the armed police and workers that will kill many people on both sides. Taking "bold social worker" action, Perkins convinces Smith that a civilized conference among all of the industrial commissioners, the copper workers, and management can alleviate the situation, and Smith calls off the state police.

Perkins then addresses the mostly Italian immigrant workers in her broken Italian. Using conferencing as a resource, she promises them to hold hearings about their grievances if they dispose of their explosives. They agree to toss the dynamite into a nearby canal. In return, Perkins talks all other commissioners into going to Rome as soon as possible. She meanwhile sounds out the workers and their employers. However, her process hits a snag when management refuses to negotiate with labor.

Perkins solves this problem in a bold if "odd social work" manner involving the conference she has set up. She learns about and attains an obscene letter that the most aggressively anti-labor factory owner, James A. Spargo, has sent to his employees, and she asks that it be read aloud at the hearing. The other employers know about the letter and publicly disassociate themselves from Spargo, earning the workers' approval and creating enough shared good will for Perkins to persuade most of the employers to negotiate. These employers secretly desire labor peace, and Perkins successfully helps negotiate an end to the strike and labor agreement. While Smith questions his faith in Perkins concerning the Rome strike, a manager of one of the copper companies requests of a state industrial commissioner, "Ask the governor where he found that woman."[13]

In the 1920s, New York elects its governors for two-year terms. In Smith's first term, the legislature passes housing regulation laws and improves workers' compensation laws. Although Smith and Perkins are turned out of office by the 1920 national Republican "return to normalcy"

DOI: 10.1057/9781137527813.0013

tide, Smith runs much better than the Democratic national ticket, and it seems likely that Smith will win the gubernatorial race in 1922, as Smith indeed does.

As a member of the Republican-reorganized Industrial Board in 1923 Perkins deals with industry code revisions and adjudicating workers' compensation cases. These tasks are well suited to her conferencing skills. Perkins gains notoriety for the even-handedness and knowledge with which she hears and decides workers' compensation cases.[14] In 1927, a *Manchester Guardian* article describes Perkins's tactful adjudication: "The people never became mere cases to her."[15]

In the last years of Smith's governorship, an anti-reform national 1920s trend again reaches New York. The New York legislature rejects an amendment to the national Constitution regulating child labor. As Perkins's thinking continues to evolve, her ability to initiate reform slows. Smith and Perkins can further social reform only in the areas already legislated. Factory inspection is thus increased, the Fifty-Four-Hour Bill in effect becomes the "Forty-Eight-Hour Bill," workers' compensation is expanded, and a "one-day-rest-in-seven" law is applied to more industries.[16]

In 1928, Governor-Elect Franklin Roosevelt surprises Perkins by asking her to serve as his chief Industrial Commissioner. As Industrial Commissioner, Perkins's investigatory social worker skills cause her to seek accurate information and statistics. Her research accuracy results in national headlines. In January 1930, Perkins reads in the *New York Times* that President Herbert Hoover says the national unemployment rate has dropped. Basing his analysis on a temporary Christmas rise in employment, Hoover's administration predicts a swift and complete economic recovery.[17] Although Hoover is perhaps accurate in the sense that there is a seasonal rise in employment, he is misleading. It should however be noted that earlier in his administration Hoover does in fact attempt to establish more accurate statistics.

Nonetheless, Perkins believes that Hoover's numbers are off. She says she is shocked and "horrified" that an ordinary worker seeking a job and not finding one would believe it is his or her fault due to Hoover's misinformation.[18] "It's a cruel deceit," she says, "because people will believe it. Mother will be mad when father comes home and says he can't get a job because the President said that unemployment is going up."[19]

Perkins puts to work her "early social work audacity." At that time, Hoover is confident that it would be difficult to refute him since

DOI: 10.1057/9781137527813.0013

unemployment is as yet a "negative" statistic derived from "positive" employment statistics. Also, the use of statistical sampling is relatively undeveloped. Unfazed, Perkins contacts an expert statistician, Simon Patton. Patton gathers statistics establishing several states' trends and interrelates them with New York data. Perkins and Patton spend a "whole day" establishing that national unemployment is definitely rising, and they report their results and methodology to the press the next day. Hoover cannot credibly rebut their conclusions.[20] Perkins's social work training teaches her to equate evidence and action, and, for Kelley and Perkins, presenting evidence and disseminating information is an important part of social work. Governor Roosevelt, in this spirit, asks her to brief him every day about labor statistics.[21] Perkins's actions as the NY Industrial Commissioner prefigure the dramatic improvement she brings to the US Bureau of Labor Statistics upon becoming the US Secretary of Labor.

On several occasions as the Industrial Commissioner in 1930, Perkins publicly corrects the Hoover administration's labor and employment statistics. In the Depression's first months, it is remarkable to the American people that a state commissioner, especially a woman state commissioner, contradicts a president's credibility.[22] Perkins becomes aware of how impertinent it appears to upstage a president, and reconsiders her actions. It is in this context that Roosevelt tells Perkins to continue acting like a social worker. As previously noted, the governor tells her, "Frances, this is the best politics you can do. Don't say anything about politics. Just be an outraged social worker and scientist."[23] Indeed, Roosevelt at times begins to sound as if he were a social worker, as in effect he becomes during to his work with the disabled in Warm Springs, Georgia. FDR encounters what it means to provide therapy and immediate assistance for polio victims who have no financial resources.

FDR's aversion to "relief" and "the dole" also factor in establishing New Deal emergency work programs. FDR realizes that simply giving Americans money will not only be simpler to administer, more quickly provide relief, and be more likely to work from the perspective of what we now think of as Keynesian compensatory spending. Roosevelt knows such direct currency dispensation would also be less expensive than work programs. Indeed, Budget Director Lewis Powell advises that instead of work programs, relief should "be in its cheapest form—direct relief."[24] However, Roosevelt avoids the appearance, in addition to what he considers the moral drawbacks, of "the dole."

DOI: 10.1057/9781137527813.0013

"To prevent starvation" and "maintain" those who "cannot" themselves do so had become, according to Roosevelt, not "charity but" "social duty."[25] Matching action to its rhetoric, the Roosevelt administration sets up the Temporary Emergency Relief Administration (TERA) in 1931, which remarkably assists 40% of New Yorkers.[26] Tellingly, FDR calls the agency *Temporary* Emergency Relief, emphasizing the limited nature of the assistance. For Roosevelt the establishment of "relief" is never something for a politician to boast about. As has been noted, Roosevelt will later consider it vital for workers to pay into social security pensions.

Evoking social work's aim of directing individuals to available resources, as New York's Industrial Commissioner, in 1930 Perkins reorganizes the state public employment offices so as to find jobs for more than ten thousand unemployed state workers.[27] In 1929, Perkins and Roosevelt anticipate the possibility of a long and severe Depression. In March 1930, they institute the Committee on Stabilization of Industry for the Prevention of Unemployment "conference." The committee is an open forum to discuss ways to prevent unemployment by stabilizing industry. This committee forecasts the National Recovery Administration three years later.

On November 13, 1930 a Committee on Stabilization of Industry for the Prevention of Unemployment report prefigures the New Deal by recommending unemployment insurance and public works programs. During Roosevelt's second two-year term between 1930 and 1931, FDR's response to the Depression alternates between the short-term remedy of the relief provided by the TERA and the long-term planning done by Perkins and the Committee on Stabilization of Industry for the Prevention of Unemployment. For this committee, Roosevelt sends Perkins to Britain, where she makes a comprehensive study of the British unemployment insurance system.

Perkins amuses FDR by telling him that British unemployment records are kept on index cards in shoe boxes stacked high in rooms with tall ceilings and accessed by very tall ladders. Perkins determines that an American system would need to differ, and she begins finding solutions for operating such a large program before computers exist. Although Perkins is more preoccupied with unemployment insurance than old-age insurance, she views them as related forms of insurance, and her plans for unemployment insurance help her in conceiving old-age pensions.

Perkins draws FDR into her planning for unemployment insurance, and when Roosevelt is elected president this planning continued on a

DOI: 10.1057/9781137527813.0013

national level leading to the Social Security Act of 1935. Perkins's work as New York's Industrial Commissioner sets the stage for her accomplishments as the US Secretary of Labor. Indeed, FDR and Perkins will give much attention to how social security is to be administered, Roosevelt sometimes teasing Perkins about the scary British ladders. Perkins eventually calls FDR from IBM's headquarters to tell the president she and IBM have worked out a reliable punch card machine system. This is the culmination of a process that started with the conferences of the New York Committee on Stabilization of Industry for the Prevention of Unemployment.

Perkins's conference method is just as valuable to the Roosevelt administration in Washington as it was in New York. For instance, as the United States Secretary of Labor during the New Deal, Perkins assesses risks associated with the chemical industry by organizing a committee of workers, employers, chemical engineers, and federal representatives, among others. The committee reaches an informed consensus making possible more intelligent government action and legislation involving workplace safety.[28] The conference method also allows Perkins to make personal contact with those whom her investigations concern and involves them in the outcomes of those investigations. Perkins believes the conference method will be her ally in "do[ing] something" about "unnecessary poverty," and in making others realize that "certain steps [are] of basic importance in lessening the personal hardships and the community burdens of unemployment and relief."[29]

As the Secretary of Labor, Perkins also frequently uses the conference method. Before officially becoming the US Labor Secretary, Perkins calls "a conference of labor leaders" to help make plans for fighting unemployment with new public works programs.[30] In 1934, Perkins institutes the Division of Labor Standards (DLS), which in effect consists of a series of educational conferences designed to disseminate information about employment opportunities, training, and working conditions from state to state. Perkins believes that spreading knowledge about employment opportunities is vital for the American worker. Through conferencing, she increasingly conveys information benefiting all facets of society. "To one who believes that really good industrial conditions are the hope for a machine civilization," writes Perkins, "nothing is more heartening than to watch conference methods and education replacing police methods."[31]

At times Perkins's social work skill-set relies less upon conferencing than on the social work skill of quickly and boldly managing available resources. This skill is exemplified by how in 1933 Perkins brings an imprecise FDR idea to life. The legislation charging the Roosevelt administration with establishing a kind of peacetime army to do important environment work, the Civilian Conservation Corps (CCC), is vaguely worded. Congress charges the president with forming and managing the CCC "under such rules and regulations as he may prescribe, and by utilizing such existing departments or agencies as he may designate."

As the Secretary of Labor, Roosevelt tasks Perkins with enrolling workers into the CCC, but she has just taken charge of a relatively inactive department with few resources available to her. Perkins asks Roosevelt how she is to deliver workers to the CCC. He tells her to "use your employment service." Perkins tells him that there now is none, and FDR asks her to "create one just like that." "Get it going quick," the President adds. When Roosevelt tells Perkins to use her "employment service," he is joking because he knows Perkins has dismantled the dysfunctional employment service she inherits from the Hoover administration. Nonetheless, she reconstitutes the US Employment Service and installs a new division to recruit CCC workers through local relief agencies. Perkins also utilizes the Forest Service to identify CCC projects and lead the recruits in accomplishing them, and the military to provide sanitary and well-functioning camps, supplies, camp infrastructure, using unemployed reserve officers as supervisors. She also concentrates on selecting recruits in their early twenties, feeling that even if they are presently undernourished they can be more quickly strengthened.

Perkins quickly solves a difficult and relatively formless problem.[32] The "employment service" within an employment service that Perkins uses as a national social work funnel to supply the CCC with needy workers is greatly expanded by her use of the same service to less selectively employ millions of Americans through FERA and the WPA.

In addition, Perkins's work for the National Recovery Administration requires both conferencing and "bold social work" skills. The NRA is a means of bringing together labor, business, and government in establishing working conditions, wages, and prices so that industry can run smoothly and spur the economy. In the NRA, business, labor, the public, and government need to find common ground through conferencing. Perkins often needs to stand boldly by the conference method in helping set NRA industry codes, as exemplified below by Perkins's role in a steel industry code public hearing in Homestead, Pennsylvania.

DOI: 10.1057/9781137527813.0013

The NRA is valuable in helping to form a ceiling over working hours and a floor under wages. The standards it sets are crucial in eventually establishing the forty-hour workweek. Also significantly reflecting conferencing values, section 7 (a) of the National Industrial Recovery Act (NIRA), which establishes the NRA, for the first time requires employers to "conference" and negotiate with unions.[33]

When the NRA is declared unconstitutional in 1935, Perkins is prepared. She has already drafted two laws necessary for saving what she most values about the NRA. The first law, the Fair Labor Standards Act of 1938, establishes minimum wage, maximum hours, and child labor provision in all federally produced, supervised, or acquired goods and services. Second, the 1935 Wagner Act guarantees the collective bargaining rights that had been in the NRA. When the Supreme Court declares the NRA unconstitutional, Perkins had already drafted early versions of the Fair Labor Standards Act and the Wagner Act. Perkins's foresight removes much of the sting from the Supreme Court's NRA decision, buoying the administration.

In 1935, when Franklin Roosevelt calls upon Perkins to draft the Social Security Act, the conference method is crucial in successfully coordinating the armies of lawyers and actuaries who are needed to generate and coherently process blizzards of statistics and legal possibilities. When the plan is nearly due to be delivered to Congress, no consensus can be reached about how to balance the roles of state and federal government in running social security. "We sat until two in the morning...the wisest thing we could do," says Perkins, "was recommend a federal-state system."[34]

The spirit of inclusiveness inherent in the conference method permeates Perkins's administrative work. For example, Perkins's ability to conference is invaluable in settling labor disputes. As Secretary of Labor, Perkins handles many conflicts between labor and management, as she had done in the 1919 Rome copper workers' strike. Perkins manages to quell disputes without police or military force. However, her prizing of conferencing, communicativeness, and conversing sometimes run counter to thinking by others in the administration. A disagreement occurs during a 1934 San Francisco Longshoremen union strike, which is supported by other striking San Francisco unions. Secretary of State Cordell Hull considers himself president while FDR is on the USS *Houston* sailing to Hawaii. Hull and Attorney General Homer Cummings insist upon sending federal troops to break the strike. Perkins

DOI: 10.1057/9781137527813.0013

meticulously monitors the San Francisco situation, and she knows US Labor Department representatives are close to negotiating a settlement. She frantically radios Roosevelt before Hull and Cummings can order military intervention or reach the president before she does.[35] When she contacts Roosevelt, he immediately stops Hull and Cummings. In fact, FDR prolongs his trip to let Perkins more effectively take the lead in resolving the strike. The President routinely lets Perkins speak for him and the administration during labor disputes.[36] FDR notably relies on Perkins to speak for the White House so as to avoid military intervention in the long General Motors sit-down strike starting Christmas day 1936.[37]

Roosevelt increasingly has confidence in Perkins's political judgment. In 1940, FDR does not declare his candidacy for an unprecedented third presidential term, and it is possible that he in fact intends not to run. However, he eventually manipulates the Democratic Party's drafting of him at its national convention in Chicago. Perkins senses more party dissension than she believes Roosevelt expects. She calls Roosevelt and tells him that party regulars feel as if he is using them. Even if the party nominates him, says Perkins, his reelection campaign could be stymied by tepid party support. She believes it crucial he come to the convention to smooth the delegates' feelings, make them feel significant, and focus their support on him.

Roosevelt tells Perkins that if he appears at the convention before his nomination he will need to promise many delegates more than he can or wishes to. However, he acknowledges a problem. FDR suggests Perkins call the first lady, Eleanor Roosevelt, to ask her to Chicago in his stead. This leads to Eleanor going to the convention, addressing it, and helping to galvanize it in Roosevelt's favor. A first lady never has spoken to a national convention before. Her address to the delegates helps curtail a protest against FDR's vice-presidential selection, Secretary of Agriculture Henry Wallace, who is a Republican and also considered too liberal. Eleanor Roosevelt's ensuring of Wallace's nomination is particularly important because FDR has already drafted a statement declining the nomination if the convention rejects Wallace.[38]

World War II presents a new state of emergency, but it does not stall Perkins's use of conference and discussion. Only eleven days after Pearl Harbor's bombing plunges the United States into World War II, Perkins organizes a major conference between powerful representatives of industry and labor. Even before Pearl Harbor, Perkins plans a conference

DOI: 10.1057/9781137527813.0013

to ease the workings between the defense industry and its workers. This conference paves the way for the unprecedented industrial output that will in large part arm the militaries of the United States and its allies and win the war. The conference also leads to the United States not suspending gains Perkins and the administration have made in workers' wages and working conditions.

During World War II, the National War Labor Board repeatedly and without exception peacefully settles labor disagreements. Although many contend that the war's increased demand necessitates lowering working condition standards and wages, Perkins counters with convincing factual evidence refuting this assumption, and the war does not degrade labor's working conditions. FDR supports Perkins. "We must accept the principle that has been established for years, that the eight-hour day is the most efficient productive day for the worker.... Protection of workers against accidents, illness, and fatigue are vital for efficiency."[39] Perkins credits FDR's "stand" for coming "through the war with basic labor legislation intact."[40]

For Perkins, the war justifies increased participation by women, minorities, the disabled, and the elderly in the workforce. The war effort after all requires everyone's participation, Perkins reasons, and she is active in promoting the notion that all should feel at home in the American workplace.[41] When the administration discusses drafting women into the military, Perkins advocates using women in the workforce instead for its postwar effect. Perkins and Eleanor Roosevelt, however, disagree about the possibility of providing defense workers quality public childcare, then a relatively novel idea, although rooted in nineteenth century rationales for kindergarten. Although Perkins is cool to the idea, the first lady's position wins out and the government establishes childcare centers.

As a means of encouraging women to join the workforce Perkins herself thinks of the name "Rosie the Riveter."[42] This is in keeping with Perkins's plans to encourage women, racial minorities, and the disabled to maintain high postwar levels of participation in the workforce.[43] Perkins's wish for all to participate in the workplace and the government again mirrors underlying conference method values. The conference method is a natural outgrowth of Perkins's training and education. Perkins claims to be informed by a lifetime she views as a conference in that she says she is merely "the product" of everyone adding "to my knowledge, to my information, and to my character."[44] Likewise for FDR, says Schlesinger, "creative government was, in part, a debate."[45]

DOI: 10.1057/9781137527813.0013

Perkins's moral compass drives her in the direction of informed yet bold, persistent action. Upon becoming the US Labor Secretary, she immediately reforms the Labor Department. The department has become rudderless. Its main preoccupation is the deportation of immigrants. Perkins investigates these deportations and finds them arbitrary, ruthless, and without merit or purpose. She discontinues them.[46] "The Labor Department didn't really do too much," says Perkins.[47] The Department of Labor, she believes, is not used to any positive end. "There had to be a disorganization of the Labor Department. I really hate to dignify it by calling it a reorganization," recalls Perkins. "The Labor Department had very little content."[48]

Ewan Clague, a 1920s US Labor Department worker who later works in Perkins's reformed Bureau of Labor Statistics (BLS), says the BLS "was a working organization in which professional stature, in the modern sense of the term, had no meaning at all."[49] Less than a decade before Perkins comes to the Labor Department, the BLS has no "professional" statisticians in the sense of statisticians trained in the social sciences by graduate schools. As Joseph Duncan and William Shelton put it in the BLS's internal history, "practical statisticians," content to record quantitative data, staff the bureau.[50] Although the Coolidge and Hoover administration begin hiring professional statisticians, during the New Deal, note Duncan and Shelton, governmental statistics change "from a clerical operation to a professional one."[51] What Duncan and Shelton call a "revolution" in government statistics utilizes probability sampling based on scrupulous mathematical analysis.[52] The professionalization of the BLS is necessary in making unemployment statistics independent and credible. Professional statistical analysis also is crucial for instituting an increasingly functional Consumer Price Index (CPI) to, for instance, measure a worker's true income.[53] The CPI later is effective in removing the politics from sensitive government issues such as social security payment cost of living adjustments. Notably, theoretical underpinnings establishing the CPI made a point of considering the woman consumer's perspective. Labor Department workers devising the CPI included women who had worked at the National Consumers League.[54]

Perkins creates the Advisory Committee to the Secretary of Labor (ACSL). Notably, the committee is composed of holdovers from Hoover's earlier attempts to reform the BLS. Under Perkins the ACSL more effectively utilizes statistical advances made in the 1920s by the American Statistical Association Committee on Government Labor Statistics.[55]

DOI: 10.1057/9781137527813.0013

According to Perkins, before her tenure, the Labor Department is "the dumping ground of all the people who were too inadequate" to work anywhere else in the federal government. However, by June 1933, the Labor Department's statistical prowess makes it a model for other departments such as Interior, Agriculture, and Commerce, and these departments join with Labor in establishing the government-wide Committee in Government Statistics and Information Services (COGSIS).[56] Duncan and Shelton observe a "conference method" mindset amongst the New Deal's statistical workers as "a heartening fraternal cohesion and interchange of ideas."[57] Significantly, ACSL and COGSIS members rise in government, providing what Thomas A. Stapleford calls "a gateway for academic experts to enter federal statistical agencies: of the fifty-seven participants in COGSIS and ACSL, twenty-six become top staff members in different federal bureaus and departments."[58]

Given the Labor Department's previous inactivity, it is groundbreaking that Perkins, as Labor Secretary, is in the forefront of the administration's first one hundred days. In addition to FDR charging Perkins with helping to develop and administer the CCC and the NRA, the Labor Department similarly works with the PWA, FERA, and the subsequent WPA.

Perkins establishes the United States Employment Service which helps to find the unemployed jobs and to counter hiring discrimination. However, Roosevelt and Perkins discover the New Deal politics of racial integration problematic, and they hesitate to integrate the CCC, for example, so as to avoid alienating influential Southern congressional members who can block their legislation. Still, Perkins appoints African Americans to executive positions within the Labor Department.[59] Notably, when Perkins becomes the US Labor Secretary, Washington is still largely segregated. Without fanfare she integrates her entire department and its cafeteria, attributing her desegregation of the lunchroom to saving workers from wasting time going out for lunch and to discouraging workers from eating in their offices and attracting insects. In fact, when Perkins becomes the Secretary of Labor she must solve a major pest control problem.[60] However, Perkins is of course much more concerned with engendering the kind of inclusive spirit animating the conference method.

In the face of opposition, Roosevelt identifies with Perkins's "bold and persistent" style and relates it to her "instinct for freedom of association" and dialogue with "common people." "You and I have the instinct

DOI: 10.1057/9781137527813.0013

for freedom of association," FDR tells Perkins in 1933. "The common people don't care about all that style, Frances, and, after all, you and I are engaged in trying to bring them into things."[61] Roosevelt is referring to an occasion when Perkins expresses audacity and openly communicative qualities in 1933 while she is holding a public hearing about the steel industry's NRA code in Homestead, Pennsylvania. Homestead's burgess, or mayor, refuses to let disgruntled steel workers and other dissenters enter the meeting. Perkins objects and tries talking with them outside in a park, but the burgess and police do not let them use the park.

Perkins quickly thinks, "We will go to the post office, there is the American flag," so they can meet on federal property. Their conference in the small and overcrowded post office eventually carries over to Washington and helps Perkins draft the NRA steel production code. Perkins explains her actions: "I had been brought up in the tradition of free speech. I took it for granted that it was the 'duty of public officers,' as Plato says, 'to listen patiently to all citizens.' "[62]

Perkins's social work skill of listening contributes to her being the only cabinet member to advise FDR against his ill-fated court-packing scheme. Because her Mount Holyoke classmate, Elizabeth Rogers, marries Supreme Court Justice Owen Roberts, Perkins knows Judge Roberts and is able to listen to him. She can tell Roberts is becoming more liberal in his views, and Roberts also leads her to believe that some of the more conservative justices are getting ready to retire.[63]

The knack of gaining significant information about the Supreme Court by acquiring the confidence of Supreme Court justices is more surprisingly on display after FDR puts Perkins in charge of crafting the Social Security Act. Two Supreme Court justices offer Perkins unusual help in securing the legislation's constitutionality at a time when the Social Security Act may meet the same fate as other New Deal legislation struck down.

Two Supreme Court justices go undercover to aid in Perkins's drafting her Social Security bill.[64] They reach out to Perkins to advise her how to craft the Social Security's unemployment insurance and old-age pensions so as to appear constitutional to progressive and conservative justices. Indirectly through his daughter, Perkins's old friend Justice Louis Brandeis offers a plan for making the Social Security Act's unemployment insurance provision constitutional. Since the Supreme Court had already sanctioned federal grants to states, Perkins adapts Brandeis's plan to fund state contributions to unemployment insurance with federal payroll taxes.[65] With Brandeis's daughter present and in all likelihood

DOI: 10.1057/9781137527813.0013

acting as a go-between for Brandeis and Perkin's lawyers, Perkins and her staff hammer out complex guidelines for implementing federal unemployment insurance programs as funds to states offsetting their social welfare expenses.[66]

Perhaps more startling is Justice Harlan Stone's direct contact with Perkins. Stone invites Perkins to a tea party at his home and asks her how things are going. She tells him that her drafting committee has "very difficult constitutional problems." Stone whispers, "The taxing power, my dear, the taxing power. You can do anything under the taxing power." Without explaining her motive to her lawyers, Perkins immediately asks them to base the Social Security Act on the federal government's power to tax.[67] Indeed, the need to make the government's taxing authority explicit in the bill makes the drafting of the Social Security Act a "hodge-podge" designed "to eliminate every possible ambiguity."[68]

The bill is ruled constitutional by a six-to-three decision. Without unusual guidance from Brandeis and Stone, perhaps deriving from Perkins's social work skills, the Social Security Act might have been declared unconstitutional. This is not to say that the fear of retribution invoked by FDR's court-packing scheme was not also instrumental in changing the voting predispositions of Justices Hughes and Roberts in their constitutional upholding of the Social Security Act and the National Labor Relations Act. If the Court had struck these measures down FDR might indeed have packed the court, as he soon would through conventional means.

Nevertheless, Perkins's social work persona and skills apparently touch or otherwise affect several Supreme Court justices. Perkins appreciates the complications of politics, she later recalls Franklin Roosevelt's political character as a "complicated nature" through which "sprang much of the drive which brought achievement," and this description mirrors Perkins's sense of social work methodology. For Perkins, social work, like Roosevelt, is "complicated," but also is a part of an enthusiastic "drive" working toward social reform.[69] Perkins thus portrays the New Deal as hinging between an artistic improvisation and a scientific experiment.[70]

Notes

1   Martin, pp. 142–144.
2   Karenna Gore Schiff, *Lighting the Way: Nine Women Who Changed Modern America* (New York, Miramax Books, 2005), p. 149.

DOI: 10.1057/9781137527813.0013

3   Downey, p. 77.
4   Martin, p. 142.
5   Ibid., pp. 142–144.
6   Coleman, p. 36.
7   Ibid.
8   Martin, pp. 165–166.
9   Ibid., p. 167.
10   Coleman, p. 38.
11   Pasachoff, pp. 44–50.
12   Downey, p. 81.
13   Ibid., pp. 81–83.
14   Martin, pp. 172–179.
15   Coleman, pp. 44–45.
16   Martin, pp. 186–195.
17   Ibid., p. 213.
18   Perkins, *Roosevelt*, pp. 95–96.
19   Downey, p. 111.
20   Perkins, *Roosevelt*, pp. 95–96.
21   Perkins, "Cooperative," p. 126.
22   Martin, p. 214.
23   Ibid., p. 218.
24   Schlesinger, vol. II, p. 289.
25   Martin, p. 219.
26   Ibid., p. 220.
27   Ibid., p. 225.
28   Cohen, p. 90.
29   Cohen, p. 84; Newman, p. 85.
30   Coleman, p. 66.
31   Perkins, "Helping," p. 624.
32   Martin, pp. 250–251.
33   Coleman, p. 76.
34   Michael Hiltzik, *The New Deal: A Modern History* (New York: Simon and Schuster, 2012) p. 246.
35   Coleman, pp. 76–77.
36   Downey, pp. 212–216.
37   Ibid., pp. 209–211.
38   Doris Kearns Goodwin, *No Ordinary Time: Franklin and Eleanor Roosevelt, The Home Front in World War II* (New York: Touchstone/Simon and Schuster, 1994), pp. 126–136.
39   Coleman, p. 102.
40   Ibid.
41   Coleman, pp. 98–101.

DOI: 10.1057/9781137527813.0013

42   Mohr, p. 31; United States Department of Labor, DOL News Brief, October
     25, 2012, http://www.dol.gov/_sec/newsletter/2012/20121025.htm#.
     UfWLzuBWJG4

43   Donald W. Whisehun, *The Human Tradition in America between the Wars,
     1920–1945* (New York: Rowman & Littlefield, 2002), p. 133.

44   Coleman, p. 49.

45   Schlesinger, vol. II, p. 289.

46   Ibid., pp. 63–64.

47   Martin, p. 110.

48   Thomas A. Stapleford, *The Cost of Living in America: A Political History of
     Economic Statistics, 1880–2000* (New York: Cambridge University Press, 2009),
     p. 148.

49   Ibid., p. 150.

50   Ibid., p. 145.

51   Ibid., p. 146.

52   Ibid., p. 168.

53   Ibid., p. 145.

54   Ibid., pp. 152–153.

55   Ibid., p. 148.

56   Ibid., p. 150–151.

57   Ibid., p. 155.

58   Ibid., p. 151.

59   Coleman, p. 65.

60   Columbia University Libraries, Part 8, p. 911.

61   Coleman, p. 65.

62   Coleman, pp. 73–74.

63   Martin, p. 388.

64   Downey, p. 235.

65   Ibid.

66   Eliot, *Recollections*, pp. 75–78.

67   Pasachoff, p. 91.

68   Eliot, *Recollections*, p. 104.

69   Perkins, *Roosevelt*, p. 3.

70   Perkins, *Roosevelt*, p. 151–173.

DOI: 10.1057/9781137527813.0013

Epilogue: The First Boondoggle Wasn't a Boondoggle—The New Deal as the Social Work of Desire and the Heart of Work

Abstract: *The epilogue also maintains that the blurring of private and public economies implicit in the New Deal characterizes ideas concerning postmodern government and society.*

▶

Keywords: Affordable Care Act; *Agrarian Justice*; Al Gore; *The Wrecking Crew*; Vietnam War

Miller, Stephen Paul. *The New Deal as a Triumph of Social Work: Frances Perkins and the Confluence of Early Twentieth Century Social Work with Mid-Twentieth Century Politics and Government.* New York: Palgrave Macmillan, 2016. DOI: 10.1057/9781137527813.0014.

DOI: 10.1057/9781137527813.0014

For Franklin Roosevelt politics is an art realized on a canvas of social work. "It was Roosevelt," says David Von Drehle, "who brought urban liberalism to its full powers, redefining the federal government as the protector of the people, not just abroad but at home, at work, in sickness, in poverty, and in old-age. He called this the New Deal."[1] Even during wartime Perkins observes post-New Deal values in FDR's work process approximating conferencing and other social work skills.

Perkins describes Roosevelt after the attack on Pearl Harbor as "sober, sincere, frank, simple, and touched with humility...and a sense of human decency." FDR "appeal[s for the White House staff and cabinet] to work together in a common cause and cancel old scores" providing "such a contrast to the screaming, arrogant, aggressive leadership of the dictators who were our enemies that its effect was immediate."[2]

For Perkins, this "leadership of the highest kind" is a culmination of social work as government that underscores "human decency" and "common cause." Such cause underlines Claudia Goldin and Robert A. Margo's analysis in *The Great Compression: The Wage Structure in the United States at Mid-Century*.[3] Goldin and Margo document how the priority the American government gives to American workers and their wages creates a precedent generating decades of post-World War II prosperity.

To speak of common cause evokes a collective responsibility to maintain individual economic rights reflecting Adolph Berle's use of Thomas Jefferson's merging of collective economic responsibility with individual political rights when Berle helps FDR craft the 1932 Commonwealth Club Address. It is perhaps significant that Berle grows up among social reformers. His father supports reform causes and as a child Berle meets Jane Addams and Lillian Wald. Berle spends time as a resident of Wald's Lower East Side Henry Street Settlement and remains devoted to Wald, as does Henry Morgenthau, Jr.

Others prominent in the New Deal do social work in addition to Frances Perkins who cuts her professional teeth at Jane Addams's Hull House and Harry Hopkins who cut his at Christodora House in New York's Lower East Side. Eleanor Roosevelt works at Lower East Side New York's Rivington Street Settlement House and investigates sweatshops for the Consumers League. In addition to Berle's and Morgenthau's early and ongoing ties to Lillian Wald and the Henry Street Settlement, Harold Ickes's involvement with social work in Chicago, which includes befriending Jane Addams and volunteering at Hull House, is instrumental in launching Ickes into national progressive politics and in eventually

DOI: 10.1057/9781137527813.0014

helping to coalesce progressive Republican and former-"Bull Moose" support for FDR in 1932.

Ickes and Perkins are the only two cabinet members to serve throughout Roosevelt's entire presidency. FDR "rejects" resignations by both Ickes and Perkins on several occasions. Roosevelt identifies with his Interior and Labor secretaries and will not let them go. Similarly, Hopkins, Morgenthau, Berle (though Berle often does not work near Roosevelt), and of course Eleanor Roosevelt are constant presences throughout FDR's entire presidency and they reflect the New Deal's ongoing engagement of social work principles.

Certainly Perkins's social work, like the work of Berle, Morgenthau, Eleanor Roosevelt, and Ickes, casts social work as government's way to assist both the poor and the wealthy by assuring a "civilized industrial society" promoting "human welfare."[4] Such a government makes the workplace a site of human growth.[5] Perkins would like a "human poten-tial" mode of thinking about the workplace to have post-Depression implications for the American workplace.

Stuart Davis, who paints jazz-inspired murals for the WPA and Federal Arts Project, says, "The artists of America do not look upon the art projects as a temporary stopgap measure, but see in them the begin-ning of a new and better day for art in this country."[6] Even within a fully employed economy Frances Perkins sees the need for government to do something like social work that fulfills similar functions as the WPA so as to employ and educate "the people who did better under the kindly prodding, the special case work, and the social supervision of the WPA projects."[7]

On the one hand Perkins recognizes the "centrifugal" (individual to collective) benefits of "centripetally" (collectively to individually) employing artists since artists contribute intuitive and innovative skills that society and government would lack without them. "Archaeologists, research workers, historians" also, says Perkins, supply unique skills. On the other hand, Perkins sees the centrifugal necessity of educating the most destitute individuals. She often juxtaposes the subject of human enrichment with aiding the destitute. Economic rights as subsistence and interaction intermingle. She notes that many "enormous" WPA projects not only enrich society and financially sustain a wide range of what we might now call cultural workers, but also provide opportunities for the personal and professional growth of cultural workers in a community setting. "The whole research and restoration of St. Augustine," Perkins

DOI: 10.1057/9781137527813.0014

recalls, "was one of the WPA projects, all done by out of work professors, students, archaeologists, and historians working together."[8]

Whereas many skilled WPA workers attain high levels of employment after the Depression in the Department of Labor and elsewhere, Perkins also notes that "you always got down to this dead level of the really poor, really depressed, who turned up in the WPA projects without having really much to bless themselves with in the way of talent."[9] The WPA also has an educational function. "A part of the work of the WPA was to develop into a program to take those women and teach them how to do something," says Perkins. "Even if it was only scrubbing, they could learn how to do superior scrubbing. So then they could be employed not only slopping around in railroad stations, but in private houses that wanted to be well-cleaned."[10] The WPA's vocational education function requires "WPAers" to work as "teachers, kindergarteners, and child care people.... However, it also requires teachers for those...who...didn't know how to do even what we think are the rudimentary necessities of a human being's life.... For the training of these women," remembers Perkins, "other WPA workers were brought in." According to Perkins, the WPA "lifted" these people "up out of just [being] dumb driven cattle and made them into people who knew how to make" and do things.[11] In being brought into an educational web, centrifugal interests are enhanced by centripetally targeted interaction with individuals.

In a sense federal World War II work programs drastically improve upon the WPA by more aggressively providing work for the disabled. Perkins notes that this is of particular interest to Roosevelt. FDR often calls Perkins to make certain the program is working. Such programs are in keeping with Roosevelt's Second Bill of Economic Rights' guarantee of meaningful work for everyone. A job bespeaks a kind of communal participation.

An artist similarly writes to Perkins, "I think it was the most thrilling thing in my life to realize that a government administration, and the President, whom I've never seen, thought that artists also were entitled to eat."[12] If Perkins views social work as an enduring and enriching activity serving everyone, the nature of such work can only be sustained by society's dynamic and mutually cooperative play between centripetal individual economic rights and centrifugal workings for the common good, and this interplay serves economic equality. Unfortunately, through the decades, the very term "social work" has taken on connotations of bureaucratic impracticality and menacing red tape so that

DOI: 10.1057/9781137527813.0014

identifying Perkins with social work may indeed undermine her historical importance. DeLysa Burnier maintains, "Representations of her profession, clothes, and body" "position" Perkins "by the popular press as a marginal governmental outsider."[13] And yet American social work begins with the impulse to restore the economic equality implicit in the initial American republic.

"Equality," as Jefferson, Madison, Adams, and to a great extent Hamilton, and other founders consider it, is at the heart of both necessary subsistence and more vitally dynamic conceptions of economic rights. If much of what now seems utopic and politically improbable about establishing greater political equality merely suggests reapplying New Deal values, these New Deal values in turn reapply those of the founders.

Are we in danger of losing our hold on New Deal values grounding what we have left of "liberal welfare government"? It is notable that all three words in "liberal welfare state" are popularly discredited, indicating the peril that general esteem for the positive values underlying government prioritizing common economic interests is in. Thomas Frank's *The Wrecking Crew* (2009) recounts right wing ideology's replacing of bipartisan acknowledgement of the permanent place of many New Deal goals and institutions within American government.[14] These New Deal institutions are subject to a purposeful sabotage of competent, cost-efficient, non-privatized government that begins under Nixon and flowers under Reagan. The disdain with which the right wing regards government makes them "by nature" inept and corrupt in such a way that government itself is undermined and its positive fruits generally sneered at as even a possibility. We see evidence of this in the difficulty most of the nation has in recognizing most of the positive outcomes of the 2010 Affordable Care Act (ACA), and if "Obamacare" did not greatly profit vast swaths of the health care industry, the ACA seems unlikely to have stood a chance. The ultimately inconsequential problems associated with the ACA's website rollout better suit a seemingly unassailable narrative concerning government incompetency than its success in providing affordable health care for millions of Americans.

Interestingly, Frank's *The Wrecking Crew* accepts the warped idea of right wing laissez faire hands-off private enterprise government as a default American economic and political position. Frank realizes such a government position is "warped" since such supposedly strong and government-free business interests require a strong government to keep to business's liking American workers and consumers and other peripheral conditions such as trade and immigration policies and actual conditions.

Nonetheless, Frank does not note that this laissez faire mindset is not one that the nation's founders or many other Americans would advocate until after the Civil War. Indeed, the corporate industrial wealth created by supplying the government during the Civil War makes such a stance impossible. The true default government and business mindsets see one another as respectful of each other and the common good. In a sense, the New Deal folds a notion of "all Americans" into the founding national economic mindset. However, will New Deal economic and political assumptions become as forgotten as those of the founders? After all, a distrust of government hits a sweet spot for both economically powerful and un-powerful right-wingers. The powerful perpetuate power, and the powerless perpetuate a sense of being better than the poor by opposing their government's assistance.

The war in Vietnam upsets the bipartisan consensus the New Deal institutionalizes. An overwhelming suspicion of government undoes a consensus respect for government that New Deal meritocracy in government engenders. A credibility gap coming from the left gives free reign for a then seemingly extinct, or in any case retrograde, far right distrust of government. Since a credibility gap allows one to doubt anything, the right and left drift into counter realities grounded in a similar object of skepticism.

From an economic perspective the governmentally unaccounted for and hidden costs of the Vietnam War cause balance of payment deficits that are new for twentieth century America and an inflation that together with the 1973 oil embargo economic slowdown produces stagflation. However, the Vietnam War causes a complementary political sense that government is inefficient and deceitful.

Roosevelt makes certain workers as well as employers and to a lesser extent government invest in Social Security so that Americans do not think of their old-age pensions and disability and unemployment insurances as government entitlements that conservatives might one day revoke. And yet when 2000 presidential candidate Al Gore speaks of safeguarding Social Security's funds in a "lockbox," Gore is an object of ridicule. We have lost our ability to understand what was once obvious. We seem to be willfully ignorant so as not to challenge the anti-government values we apparently prefer to accept uncritically. We have

DOI: 10.1057/9781137527813.0014

become paradoxically authoritarian and anti-government, suspecting government's role in protecting social welfare.

A de facto disrespect for government also meets the New Deal in the 1930s. New Deal opponents sneer at the WPA by noting that one of the products a small western WPA project makes are "boondoggles," which is simply a western term for cowboy gadgets and saddle trappings. The first boondoggle is not a boondoggle! Indeed, conservative think tanks and bloggers now call "Social Security a boondoggle of biblical proportions."[15] Another celebrated non-scandal scandal occurs in 1939 when conservative congress members nearly impeach Perkins for not deporting International Longshore and Warehouse Union leader Henry Bridges, who immigrated from Australia, at a time when the Labor Department controls deportations. With little evidence, Bridges is believed to be a communist. Although Perkins enforces federal deportation laws, she is widely believed to ignore a nonexistent law.

In fact, Perkins "end[s] the corruption at the Bureau of Immigration," says DeLysa Burnier.[16] Perkins's competency in the Bridges matter reflects her wider competency in making the BLS and the Division of Labor Standards work. Indeed, according to Burnier, "Members of congress, though, never forgive her" for her efficiency and competence since she "made it clear that Labor would no longer be a clearinghouse for congressional patronage."[17] Congress thus denies adequate funding for the US Federal Employment Service.

Tellingly, New Deal opponents publicize anything that merely sounds like a scandal because the New Deal is virtually scandal-free. New Deal programs are well administered. Indeed, although the Affordable Care Act website mishaps are relatively minor, it is difficult to find corresponding New Deal small-scale calamities. Perkins and Roosevelt personally sweat the details about how unprecedented recordkeeping and payment and benefit Social Security procedures will operate. She personally goes to IBM headquarters to help in the planning of social security procedures that she correctly assures FDR will work. Similarly, Roosevelt, knowing government work programs are assumed to be corrupt, takes unusual precautions to guard against corruption in the WPA, PWA, and other work programs. The president assigns Ickes with overseeing the WPA and the PWA financing because Ickes is relentless in safeguarding against all manner of fraud and fiscal dishonesty. All of the thousands of papers concerning money and appropriations must pass Ickes's intense scrutiny. And Ickes's snoopy supervision does not end there. At the cost

DOI: 10.1057/9781137527813.0014

of his personal likability, Ickes constantly monitors and investigates for any possibility of misused funds. At a meeting of WPA administrators, Roosevelt notes that the absence of any major scandals in the WPA is no small feat.

"The most common and durable source of factions has been the various and unequal distribution of property," says James Madison in the Tenth Federalist Paper. "Those who hold and those who are without property," continues Madison, "have ever formed distinct interests in society. Those who are creditors, and those who are debtors, fall under a like discrimination. A landed interest, a manufacturing interest, a mercantile interest, a moneyed interest, with many lesser interests, grow up of necessity in civilized nations, and divide them into different classes, actuated by different sentiments and views. The regulation of these various and interfering interests forms the principal task of modern legislation, and involves the spirit of party and faction in the necessary and ordinary operations of the government."[18] Clearly, the founders foresee what FDR in 1936 calls the "dangers" of "organized money" that "considers the Government of the United States as a mere appendage to their own affairs."[19] The founders, much like Perkins and FDR, do not arbitrarily separate economic and political rights.

One hundred and thirty years before Oliver Wendell Holmes, Jr. writes, "a discouragement may be part of an encouragement when seen in its organic connection with the whole. Taxes are what we pay for civilized society, including the chance to insure,"[20] and 138 years before Frances Perkins responds to the Senate Finance Committee question, "Does the proposal involved in this legislation seek, in any sense, to substitute social security for the struggle for existence?" by saying, "cooperation between individuals has accounted for as much civilization as any personal struggle; most of us have tried to give a certain security to those who are dependent upon us from the more serious aspect of the struggle for existence, and to a very large extent we have succeeded in civilizing society. That is the purpose of civilization,"[21] Thomas Paine prefigures Holmes and Perkins by devising reason for and methodology to use social insurance and progressive taxation to "civilize" the advanced yet inhuman "civilizations" of his time. In 1796, Paine writes the pamphlet "Agrarian Justice."[22]

Although Paine is then living in France, "Agrarian Justice" is not "for any particular country." It is rather "a little work" within the "new study" of "the rights of man." Paine opposes the idea of government as "nothing

DOI: 10.1057/9781137527813.0014

more at heart than to maintain courtiers, pensioners, and all their train, under the contemptible title of royalty...by showing that society is aiming at a very different end—maintaining itself."

As Paine's notion of government is self-propelling and requires no pomp, Social Security as Perkins, Roosevelt, and others in the New Deal shape it is pay-as-you-go. The program has no authority to borrow money. Outright propaganda exaggerates the small problems involved with small expected shortfalls several decades hence that would in any case later self-correct but might require a small quite fixable adjustment for the "short term" to correspond with the underlying "long term." It is remarkable what dupes otherwise reliable journalists have been in this regard.

For instance, in a 2008 presidential debate, Tom Brokaw calls Social Security "a big ticking time bomb that will eat us,"[23] and in a 2012 vice-presidential debate Martha Raddatz says Social Security is "going broke."[24] In fact, Social Security needs absolutely no readjustments to pay full benefits until 2033.[25] And yet even this piece of information does not begin to convey the solidity of social security's foundation. First, Social Security is financed by taxes on workers and employers, returns on government bonds bought with surplus Social Security funds, and taxes paid by Social Security recipients. So what could Martha Raddatz or anyone else mean by Social Security "going broke"? This is absurd! As long as people, including Social Security recipients, pay taxes, and the United States pays interest on its bonds, Social Security cannot go broke. Second, what could it mean for Social Security to go broke? Other government agencies would automatically go broke without government funding. However, Social Security is a self-funding mechanism. We expect much more from Social Security than other government functions, bureaus, and departments. The very manageable shortfall Social Security actuaries responsibly warn us about could be easily managed if responsible journalists such as Raddatz owned up to their embarrassing gullibility and informed instead of misled the public. Social Security could only go bankrupt if it was abolished by Congress. A simple way to fix the 2033 estimated shortfall would be doing away with the cap on paying taxes for income over $117,000.[26] Numerous other easy fixes are possible.

It is remarkable that Social Security has survived "starve-the-beast stealth attacks on the program's budget."[27] Although these "anti-social security forces" have managed to delay benefits and to inconvenience

DOI: 10.1057/9781137527813.0014

and unreasonably harass Social Security recipients, the program has not been undermined because Social Security is designed so efficiently that it only uses 1% of its revenues on administration.[28]

Paine's program would have required property and inheritance taxes since, says Paine in *Agrarian Justice*, "It is wrong to say God made rich and poor; He made only male and female, and He gave them the earth for their inheritance." In 1787, Jefferson similarly writes to Madison, "Whenever there are in a country uncultivated lands and unemployed poor, it is clear that the laws of property have been so far extended as to violate the natural right. The earth is given as a common stock for man to labor and live on." He writes, "If for the encouragement of industry we allow it to be appropriated, we must take care that other employment be provided for those excluded from the appropriation. If we do not, the fundamental right to labor the earth returns to the unemployed."[29] The land that in effect belongs to all, says Paine, is essentially responsible for individual wealth. Paine notes that no one person alone can create great wealth. Thus Paine would impose a 10% tax upon land and inheritance. In England he calculates that this would raise £5,666,666. This would fund both those over fifty and the disabled with £10 annually. Since an average British laborer earned approximately twice this amount annually, Paine's program perhaps would provide something in the range of what we consider minimum wage today, about what American old-age Social Security pensioners receive.

Remarkably, Paine's social insurance architecture also anticipates something much like student loan grants. Paine's fund would provide those turning twenty-one years old with a one-time payment of fifteen pounds to learn a trade and/or establish themselves in its practice. Paine justifies these payments by: "taking it then for granted that no person ought to be in a worse condition when born under what is called a state of civilization, than he would have been had he been born in a state of nature, and that civilization ought to have made, and ought still to make, provision for that purpose, it can only be done by subtracting from property a portion equal in value to the natural inheritance it has absorbed."[30] Similarly those whose health suffers from working for landed property holders should be compensated. Clearly, FDR's identification of the New Deal with America's founders is no mere rhetorical sleight of hand.

In the third television season of *House of Cards* in 2015, fictional president Francis Underwood, portrayed by Kevin Spacey, makes an unemployment-fighting government work program he calls America

DOI: 10.1057/9781137527813.0014

Works the centerpiece of the coming presidential election. In the television show, the work program's first rollout is surprisingly popular. President Underwood invokes the New Deal by paying tribute to FDR at his memorial in Washington and citing Roosevelt's imperative to engage in bold and persistent experiment. And yet the fictional president's bold idea is to act on the fictive misinformation that Social Security contributes to budget deficits. Underwood's experiment is to demolish Social Security pensions and jettison Roosevelt's institutional and philosophical works aimed at guaranteeing economic rights and security to pay for "America Works." Roosevelt, to the contrary, conducts the world's first governmental experiment in compensatory deficit spending to finance the New Deal's emergency work programs. However, America Works, unlike the WPA, merely provides funds to private corporations to hire the unemployed. There is thus none of the CCC's, WPA's, PWA's, and other New Deal work programs' lasting contributions that are made independently from the prime motive of profit. Although the PWA does not directly hire workers, it backs projects such as San Francisco's Bay Bridge, the Lincoln Tunnel, thousands of streets and schools and post offices and sewer systems and universities and canals and hospitals, and the electrification of much of rural America for these projects' contribution to the national welfare and their "multiplier effect" stimulating other jobs in the economy. And yet no other *House of Cards* fictional presidential candidate goes so far as to espouse any economic remedies that even approach the progressive aspect of America Works—in itself a mere shadow of the more progressive aspects of actual New Deal work programs. Put simply, the economic solutions Frances Perkins, Franklin Roosevelt, and the New Deal put forward are stranger than fiction, even fiction more than eighty years in the future—even when that fiction claims the high ground of the New Deal's legacy.

It is no accident that *House of Cards* finds both its political resources (work programs) and limits (cutting Social Security pensions) in the New Deal. After World War II, we create the kind of consumption-driven society anticipated by basic Jeffersonian, Hamiltonian, Scottish Enlightenment, and Keynesian assumptions in favor of the circulation of economic value. "I think you may be overlooking the difference between income and wealth," Perkins says to the 1935 Senate Committee's objections to the idea that Social Security could improve the economy. "Income," says Perkins, "arises from the velocity with which the medium of exchange moves from hand to hand, whereas wealth, of course, is

DOI: 10.1057/9781137527813.0014

more solid and substantial."[31] We have also not passed beyond the New Deal's economic assumptions since we have institutionalized much that saves us. Social Security pensions, Medicare, Medicaid, disability and unemployment insurance, progressive income taxes, and food stamps prevent a full-scale depression after the 2008 economic collapse by keeping consumer demand and the economy afloat.[32]

However, we are caught within a misinterpretation of the New Deal's Keynesian legacy. Whereas Roosevelt spurs the economy through World War II deficit spending, he also as Keynes would have had it accounts for this spending with unprecedented progressive tax measures assuring the future management of the national debt in the crucial sense of limiting the debt to a manageable and relatively stable fraction of the Gross Domestic Product. The national debt only begins to get uncomfortable with Johnson's unplanned Vietnam War spending that becomes markedly more cumbersome with Nixon's tax cuts, and begins to spiral with Reagan's larger tax cuts.

Reasonably progressive taxes are an offsetting side of Keynesian compensatory deficit spending. If taxes are not drastically cut in good times, an economy routinely and painlessly pays for its previous government stimulation. George W. Bush's tax cuts are precisely what not to do. This is especially what not to do when engaging in wars of choice. Nothing could be less in accord with FDR's wise if "unconscious" understanding of Keynes. Roosevelt could be speaking for Keynes when he speaks of "flatten[ing] out the peaks and valleys" of the economy.[33] If war spending itself might stimulate the economy, Roosevelt knows that such stimulation would be inadequate without a responsible tax program. Conversely, LBJ and Nixon irresponsibly stimulate the economy and produce postwar stagflation to fund the Vietnam War, requiring Jimmy Carter and Paul Volcker to begin draining the inflationary Vietnam War spending from the economy, which is finally accomplished in the 1980s. It is as if World War II's comparative strength of purpose and relative transparency as opposed to the Vietnam and early twenty-first century wars' apparent aggressive misinformation campaigns are reflected in the economic lives and aftermaths of these wars.

We also live within the confines of the New Deal because of what FDR calls its social insurance "structure," which FDR seems to expect the future Americans to build upon. Roosevelt calls the 1935 Social Security Act "in short, a law that will take care of human needs and at the same time provide for the United States an economic structure of vastly greater

DOI: 10.1057/9781137527813.0014

soundness."[34] In fact, Medicare and Medicaid are 1960s extensions of the 1935 Social Security Act. Similarly, the Social Security Administration administers the Supplemental Nutrition Assistance Program (SNAP), more commonly known as Food Stamps. More recently, the 2010 Affordable Care Act has extended Medicaid eligibility.

As I write in April 2015 the expansion of Social Security may be shaping up as the chief social and economic justice initiative of the 2016 election. (However, as I proof this immediately after the November 13, 2015 Paris terrorist attacks, it seems that exaggerated links between immigration and terrorism might alter the election.) How odd that a 1935 program still guides our efforts for making social progress. Perhaps we can understand why this is by using a modernist model of development. Theodore Roosevelt's New Nationalism introduces modern government as a powerful idea. However, it is a powerful modernist idea isolated from everyday experience. Perkins and FDR's New Deal brings the New Nationalism down to earth.

If we are in a "postmodern" period of history what might this have to do with the New Deal? We have come to associate postmodernism with a late capitalist end of history. It seemed that it was relentlessly liquid capital and not socialism that could afford to see government wither away. And yet that no longer appears to be the case. The kernel of the New Nationalism fructifies as the New Deal and may ultimately expand rather than vanish in postmodern society. After all, what does postmodernism mean if not a blurring of figure and background arising from the connectivity of everything in contemporary culture? Within this mixing and blurring are not Paine's "Agrarian Justice" fund, TR's New Nationalism, Martin Luther King Jr's sixties formulation of the New Deal and economic rights, and a future New Deal, related to this connectivity?

And yet this is contingent upon a political desire for economic freedom. FDR asks Frances Perkins to head the Committee on Economic Security drafting the Social Security Act of 1935 because he says Perkins sincerely cares about social security and she is thus the most likely member of his administration to see it through to its enactment, and Frances Perkins similarly emphasizes political desire by describing a political party as "a sort of tasting of each other's personalities, each other's bent of mind and habit of thought, and particularly each other's emotional reactions." She explains the import of emotion in her decision to drop her apolitical stance and become a Democrat in 1920. "It is out of the emotions that

DOI: 10.1057/9781137527813.0014

people form their political philosophy. They're only slightly influenced by their intellectual and logical convictions," says Perkins. "It's what they want reinforced, if they are wise and temperate at all, by what their intellect, their knowledge and their logic teaches them. But if they don't desire it deeply in an emotional way, they'll never set upon it."[35] Frances Perkins desires a New Deal before FDR and America need one.

Notes

1   Von Drehle, p. 263.
2   Perkins, *Roosevelt*, p. 368.
3   http://www.nber.org/papers/w3817.pdf
4   Perkins, "Helping," p. 630.
5   Coleman, p. 18.
6   Richard D. McKinzie, *The New Deal for Artists* (Princeton, NJ: Princeton University Press, 197), p. 250.
7   Perkins, *Roosevelt*, pp. 189–190.
8   Columbia University Libraries, Part 4, pp. 528–530.
9   Ibid.
10 Ibid.
11 Ibid.
12 Ibid., p. 523.
13 DeLysa Burnier, "Frances Perkins' Disappearence from American Public Administration: A Geneology of Marginalization," *Administrative Theory and Praxis*, 30:4 (December 2008), 398–423: 411.
14 Thomas Frank, *The Wrecking Crew: How Conservatives Ruin Government, Enrich Themselves, and Better the Nation.* (New York, Holt, 2009).
15 http://www.answerbit.com/money-deducted-from-social-security- check-to-cover-insu-20100816114653AAw3JRr (accessed January 16, 2014)
16 Burnier, p. 407.
17 Ibid.
18 http://www.constitution.org/fed/federa10.htm
19 http://docs.fdrlibrary.marist.edu/od2ndst.html
20 http://caselaw.lp.findlaw.com/cgi-bin/getcase. pl?court=us&vol=275&invol=870
21 www.ssa.gov/history/pdf/s35perkins.pdf, p. 129.
22 http://piketty.pse.ens.fr/files/Paine1795.pdf
23 http://www.cnn.com/2008/POLITICS/10/07/presidential.debate.transcript/
24 http://www.debates.org/index.php?page=october-11-2012-the-biden-romney-vice-presidential-debate

DOI: 10.1057/9781137527813.0014

25   *New York Times* (October 2, 2014), p. A31, http://www.nytimes.
      com/2014/10/02/opinion/gail-collins-securing-social-security.html
26   Ibid.
27   Nancy Altman and Eric Kingston, *Social Security Works!: Why Social Security
      Isn't Going Broke and How Expanding It Will Help Us All* (New York: The New
      Press, 2015), p. 197.
28   Ibid.
29   Thomas Jefferson to James Madison, February 1787. Philip S. Foner, ed.,
      Thomas Jefferson: Selections from His Writings, pp. 56–57. http:// www.let.rug.nl/
      usa/presidents/thomas-jefferson/letters-of-thomas-jefferson/ jefl41.php
30   http://www.ssa.gov/history/paine4.html
31   www.ssa.gov/history/pdf/s35perkins.pdf, p. 130.
32   James K. Galbraith, p. 187.
33   http://www.presidency.ucsb.edu/ws/?pid=14916
34   Ibid.
35   Columbia University Libraries, Part 2, p. 49.

DOI: 10.1057/9781137527813.0014

Index

DOI: 10.1057/9781137527813.0015

CPSIA information can be obtained
at www.ICGtesting.com
Printed in the USA
LVOW11*0228060317
526239LV00002B/33/P